CONCILIUM

CONCILIUM
ADVISORY COMMITTEE

Regina Ammicht-Quinn, Deutschland
María Pilar Aquino, USA
Mile Babić OFM, Bosna i Hercegovina
José Oscar Beozzo, Brasil
Wim Beuken, Belgique
Maria Clara Bingemer, Brasil
Leonardo Boff, Brasil
Erik Borgman OP, Nederland
Christophe Boureux OP, France
Lisa Sowle Cahill, USA
John Coleman, USA
Eamonn Conway, Ireland
Mary Shaw Copeland, USA
Enrico Galavotti, Italia
Dennis Gira, France
Norbert Greinacher, Deutschland
Gustavo Gutiérrez OP, Perú
Hille Haker, USA
Hermann Häring, Deutschland
Linda Hogan, Ireland
Diego Irrarázaval CSC, Chile
Werner G. Jeanrond, Sweden
Jean-Pierre Jossua OP, France
Maureen Junker-Kenny, Ireland
François Kabasele Lumbala RD, Congo
Hans Küng, Deutschland
Karl-Joseph Kuschel, Deutschland
Nicholas Lash, United Kingdom
Solange Lefebvre, Canada
Mary-John Mananzan, Philippines
Daniel Marguerat, Suisse

Alberto Melloni, Italia
Norbert Mette, Deutschland
Johann-Baptist Metz, Deutschland
Dietmar Mieth, Deutschland
Jürgen Moltmann, Deutschland
Paul D. Murray, United Kingdom
Sarojini Nadar, South Africa
Teresa Okure, Nigeri
Agbonkhianmeghe Orobator SJ, Kenya
Aloysius Pieris SJ, Srī Lankā
Susan A. Ross, USA
Giuseppe Ruggieri, Italia
Léonard Santedi Kinkupu RD, Congo
Silvia Scatena, Italia
Paul Schotsmans, België
Elisabeth Schüssler Fiorenza, USA
Jon Sobrino SJ, El Salvador
Janet Martin Soskice, United Kingdom
Luiz Carlos Susin OFM, Brasil
Elsa Tamez, Costa Rica
Christoph Theobald SJ, France
Andrés Torres Queiruga, España
David Tracy, USA
Marciano Vidal, España
João J. Vila-Chã SJ, Portugal
Marie-Theres Wacker, Deutschland
Elain M. Wainwright, New Zealand
Felix Wilfred, India
Ellen van Wolde, Nederland
Christos Yannarás, Ελλαδα
Johannes Zizioulas, Türkiye.

CONCILIUM 2020/3

Politics, Theology and the Meaning of Power

Edited by

Michelle Becka, Bernarderth Caero Bustillos,
João Vila-Chã

Published in 2020 by SCM Press, 3rd Floor, Invicta House, 108–114 Golden Lane, London EC1Y 0TG.

SCM Press is an imprint of Hymns Ancient & Modern Ltd (a registered charity) 13A Hellesdon Park Road, Norwich NR6 5DR, UK

Copyright © International Association of Conciliar Theology, Madras (India)

www.concilium-vatican2.org

English translations copyright © 2020 Hymns Ancient & Modern Ltd.

All rights reserved. No part of this publication may be reproduced, stored in a retrieval system, or transmitted, in any form or by any means, electronic, mechanical, photocopying or otherwise, without the prior written permission of the Board of Directors of Concilium.

ISBN 978-0-334-05958-5
Printed in the UK by
Ashford, Hampshire

Concilium is published in March, June, August, October, December

Contents

Editorial

The Subjunctive Power of God
JOHN D. CAPUTO 12

The Inter-Action of Power and Authority:
The Force of the Symbol and the Strengthening of Reality
JOÃO J. VILA-CHÃ 22

Power As Service:
A Critical Reading of Power from the New Testament
IVONI RICHTER REIMER & HAROLDO REIMER 32

Empowerment of the Disempowered:
Some Glimpses into Jesus' Life and Mission
A. MARIA ARUL RAJA 42

The Power of the Law – the Law of Power:
On the Significance of Canon Law for Issues of Power in the Church
JUDITH HAHN 52

From the New Political Theology to Critical Political Ethics
HILLE HAKER 63

Discursive, Socio-Economically Sensitive and Performative:
Varieties of Publicly Political Christianity
ANSGAR KREUTZER 74

Theology and the Power of Liberation
FRANCISCO DE AQUINO JÚNIOR   85

Protesting Patriarchal Power:
The Task of Political Theology in Creating Solidarity and Sustaining
Activism
TANYA VAN WYK   94

Power Dynamics Beyond Collusion and Resistance:
"The Catholic Philippines" as Privileged Locus
JOSE MARIO C. FRANCISCO   105

Passion Consistent With the Depth of the Wounds of the Oppressed
LAREINE-MARIE MOSELY, SND   118

Theological Forum
Synodality – in Practice
NORBERT METTE   128

Contributors   135

Editorial

'The political dimension of the faith is nothing other than the Church's response to the demands made upon it by the de facto socio-political world in which it exists'
(Archbishop Romero, Address on receiving an honorary doctorate from the University of Louvain, Belgium, 2 February 1980).

But how do we discern the challenge(s), and what are the answers? In the wake of the Second Vatican Council theologians in various places, including this journal, have tried to explore the idea of a theology in the social context of a particular period.[1] According to Metz, both the privatisation of religion and its reactionary politicisation within existing political systems contradict the Christian message. Instead, we must use critical reason to plumb its depths again and again to see how 'the eschatological message of Christianity must be formulated under the conditions of a structurally altered public sphere'.[2] Theology is located in society and contains a social-critical potential. Today once more, in changing public spheres, this claim must be maintained, updated and examined. This issue of *Concilium* makes a contribution to that task.

Is theology allowed to be political – or if it is does it lose all claim to objectivity and ultimately its scientific character? Can theology be non-political – or isn't any option or position, which will necessarily be made or taken, already political? These and other questions, which anyway cannot be given a clear answer, are raised in different regional contexts in very different ways. Political systems, but also the varying sense of what theology is – embedded as it may be in state or Church institutions – determine the relationship of theology and politics and produce varying ideas of power. The political aspects of theology and the role of theology in politics are complex and often ambivalent. As a result this issue of *Concilium* brings together very varied perspectives and contexts –

Editorial

political, regional, denominational and from different specialist fields of theology. They are placed side by side. If this produces tensions, that is quite deliberate.

At the centre is the relationship of theology and politics – and the issue of the role of power. The issue is not new and yet, given current political developments across the world, reflection on this topic is an urgent necessity. For example, among the great challenges revealed are the revival of authoritarian regimes, the questioning of the system in existing democracies and the instrumentalisation of religion.

The Church has always been faced with the question of what its relation should be to the power of the state – often enough it has tried to get close to it, to get a share of power for itself. What role did and does theology play then? It can attempt to legitimate the lust for power of particular parties or regimes or adopt a critical position towards secular power and protest against it. By what criteria does this take place, and can inadmissible confrontations and the construction of new enemy figures be avoided? In many of the essays collected here the power of theology – and that of religion and the Church – is represented as 'different' from that of the dominant power. A variety of reflections consider what this difference consists of, and how it can be prevented from itself becoming uncontrolled and violent.

Some contributions consider the area of politics that goes beyond institutional politics: in the shaping of society Christians – whether they explicitly identify as such or not – are central actors. As part of civil society, for example, they take part in political movements. They shape political power; and it is the task of theology to identify this activity (as faith-based activity and political activity) and examine it. The very different contributions contained in this issue agree in the assumption that this political activity resulting from faith must be a liberating activity, which not only sees and takes account of the sufferings of the most deprived, but also sees its aim as the reduction of suffering and a commitment to greater justice.

Theological discussion of power and the definition of the relationship of theology and politics cannot be separated from the Church's exercise of power. The Church is not outside society; rather, it is part of civil society and so of politics. Particularly in view of abuse within the Church, the

Editorial

question must constantly be raised of how the Church exercises power and whether ways of discussing and monitoring this exist, and what they are. This issue is also one of the topics discussed in the articles.

To start us off, John Caputo asks what ruling is like in the kingdom of God. With Paul against Paul he identifies the power of God as one which is not only greater than any human power but also a non-violent force. The result is a call for rule without violence as an imperative for Christians.

João J. Vila-Chã explains the interrelation of authority and power as a constitutive element of human existence. He emphasises the relational character of authority and power, and shows that both must be limited if they are not to be misused, but can be redemptive. While in political society this takes place through consistent respect for the constitution and the rule of law, in the Church it remains indivisibly linked with personal, loyal obedience to the incarnate Son of God.

In the first of the following two New Testament articles Ivoni Richter Reimer and Haroldo Reimer consider the concept of power in New Testament texts. These reveal various ideas of power and rule, but they are frequently concepts of counter-power. This also applies to the idea of the kingdom of God, which implies a relational concept of power. This power is linked to service and so turns traditional ideas on their head. The article explains what service looks like in the New Testament texts and draws conclusions about a liberating view of rule and power in the early Church.

Maria Arul Raja portrays Jesus' understanding of power and authority as illustrated in attitudes and actions. Typical features of this concept of power are the protection and promotion of life in opposition to the violence of the system. This shows central aspects of his discussion of power to be an ethics of egalitarianism, an aesthetics of solidarity, and a new power to become human.

Next Judith Hahn investigates power in canon law. She explains the power of law, because law has a central role in establishing societies. And she explains the law of power, because that is about the creation of authority. The central question then is how this power is to be limited. In modern states it is law again that sets limits to power. But it is precisely here that some questions arise about canon law. The article explains these and reveals some blind spots.

Hille Haker's article links an approach to political theology with a critical political ethics. In this, solidarity with those who suffer is both a moral criterion of judgment and a guide to action for Christians in personal and political life. Haker goes on to show that there are four different dimensions of freedom to be considered and guaranteed if liberation from suffering and oppression is not itself to produce injustice. On this basis she outlines a theological ethics that is a critical political ethics, which listens to the voices of experience and is constructive and creative.

Ansgar Kreutzer focuses on the practice of Political Night Prayer, widespread in Germany since the 1960s. He directs his attention to the combination produced in this practice of detailed discussion of political issues on the one hand and Christian symbolic practices in a liturgical framework on the other. By drawing on concepts of the public sphere from the social sciences, he points to the significance of not only discursive, but also performative, elements for the politics in the public sphere that a Christianity that also sees itself as engaged in politics in the public sphere can make use of.

Francisco de Aquino Júnior addresses the liberating force of theology from a Brazilian perspective. The link with a liberating faith (faith and liberation) makes theology itself a force for liberation. In this way both the intellectual specificity of theology and its character as an element of faith are both emphasised.

Tanya van Wyk discusses the relationship between ruling, power and theology from a gender perspective, because political theologies are necessarily contextual theologies – and so also determined by gender identity. The exercise of power can take the form of violence against women, and simultaneously there are also protest movements against this violence. Wyk discusses these and asks how far they change power structures in which women often are not involved. In this context political theology must contribute to creating awareness, condemn dehumanising practices and influence an alternative concept of power.

The particular situation of the Philippines determines José Mário Francisco's perspective on power and resistance. Catholics could be found in both political camps, either connected with or in opposition to the ruling establishment. This essay's critical analysis goes beyond binary relationships and gives us a dense description of the dynamics affecting the symbolic, institutional and allied powers of Philippine Catholicism.

Editorial

Popular devotion and political commitment come together and lead to complex theological discoveries, which the author explains.

From the perspective of black theology, LaReine-Marie Mosely places the oppressed at the centre of her article. She asks what relationship the Church has with the oppressed, and makes this specific in a critique of two bishops' assemblies – one from around 150 years ago and one from 2019. This raises the question of who is named and so recognised as particularly oppressed and vulnerable. She accuses the bishops of missing opportunities because in fact people oppressed in many ways were not named. In the light of this the author calls for a synodal Church that denounces injustice and exclusion for what it is – in a creative and responsible way.

In the Theological Forum Norbert Mette takes up the current hot topic of the synodal character of the Church. In a historical review he goes back to the synods or assemblies with a synodal character that took place in central Europe in the 1960s and 1970s. A common concern of these meetings was, starting from the decisions of the Second Vatican Council, to take seriously the responsibility of the whole people of God for the mission of the Church, and to look for directions and signposts for a renewal of local Church life that would equip it to face the future. The article explains the courses of action chosen and the results sought.

This issue of *Concilium* discusses the relationship of power, rule and theology from the perspective of different disciplines and regions. Questions are raised, problems exposed and challenges identified. They need further work, more detailed description and deeper analysis, all of which will necessarily look different in different place. To these theological reflections *Concilium* in this issue would like to offer encouragement and a welcome.

Michelle Becka, Bernardeth Caero Bustillos, Joaõ Vila-Chã

Translated by Francis McDonagh

Notes

1. Cf Johann Baptist Metz, 'Das Problem einer "politischen" Theologie und die Bestimmung der Kirche als Institution gesellschaftskritischer Freiheit', in: *Concilium* 4/1968, 403-411.
2. Johann Baptist Metz, 'Das Problem einer "politischen" Theologie und die Bestimmung der Kirche als Institution gesellschaftskritischer Freiheit', 403-411.

The Subjunctive Power of God

JOHN D. CAPUTO

In what sense does the basileia tou theou *rule or have power? In Christianity, Jesus is the icon of the invisible God. In Jesus, whose life is marked by compassion and forgiveness, we have an intuition of the divine order, but one in which, unlike the deities of Greece and Rome, he does not crush his enemies but is defeated by them. In 1 Cor 1, Paul captures this: the weakness of God is stronger than human strength. Stronger in what sense? Paul's answer in 1 Cor 2 is divine violence, apocalyptic power. I argue that 1 Cor 2 compromises 1 Cor 1. The true power of God lies in the unconditional call for a kingdom without force, even celestial force, where the kingdom means what the world would look like if God ruled. The true power of God is subjunctive, and it is up to us to make that kingdom come true.*

The translation of the New Testament Greek *basileia tou theou* as the "kingdom" or "reign" of God has become controversial these days. Feminists object to the gender – a king, not a queen – and either way, king or queen, the image of reigning royalty brushes against the grain of the citizens of modern democracies, who distrust images of top-down power. The sovereignty of God easily translates into earthly political sovereigns. This is not just a translation problem. It forces us to ask, what is the power of God? Is it inseparable from divine sovereignty? How are we to think it?

We do not want to give up on power altogether. When people are disempowered – the poor and persecuted, immigrants and exiles, the third world, racial and ethnic minorities, women – justice demands that they be empowered. That is the cry of the prophets: to empower the powerless. Even the word "hospitality" makes reference to power, the power (*posse, potens*) to welcome the *hostis*, the stranger. I cannot make the other welcome in someone else's home. It must be my home, where I am the proprietor and the one taking the risk. I must be in the position to say welcome.

We don't want to be weak about true power. We want hospitality to be stronger than hostility. We would like to think that love has real power, and that the power of love is greater than the power of hatred and aggression. The New Testament expression is referring to what the world would look like if God ruled, if true power held sway, and not the "powers and principalities," the evildoers, who represent the reign of brute force, which in this case meant the brutal *imperium Romanum*. We want God's power, the power of the good, to be stronger that the powers and principalities, the power of evil. So we need to distinguish *the divinity of true power* in the kingdom, the power of the truly divine, from *the profanity of mere force*, which cannot be God's power.

I 1 Cor 1.

The paradoxical thing about Christianity is that, unlike the Greek and Roman divinities, unlike almost any divinity, the mark of the divine, of the true power of God, is found in what for all the world is weakness. In one of the most explosive texts in the New Testament, Paul writes:

> For the foolishness of God is wiser than human wisdom, and the weakness of God (*to asthenes tou theou*) is stronger than human strength...But God chose what is weak in the world to shame the strong; God chose what is low and despised in the world, things that are not (*ta me onta*), to reduce to nothing the things that are (*ta onta*). (1 Cor 1:25, 27-28)

Against the Greek philosophers of Corinth, who advance the cause of wisdom, power, and being, Paul announces the counter-principle of the cross, of folly, weakness, and nullity. In speaking of *"ta me onta,"* the non-beings, the nothings and nobodies, Paul uses an expression that would have scandalized the philosophers, that would have been foolishness (*moria*) to them. Paul is confronting head-on the elite, the powers that *be* (*ta onta*), the men of substance (*ousia*), with the scandal of the cross. For them, this is sheer nonsense. For Luther, this is the logic of the cross, where the revelation that takes place in the New Testament is made *sub contraria specie*, under the appearance of the opposite, according to which what is foolish is wise and what is weak is strong and what is null and void enjoys real being.

Paul says he did not meet Jesus in the flesh but his words to the Corinthians ring true to what we know of Jesus. The kingdom whose coming Jesus announced turned on a logic, or a logic of amazing reversals, of paradoxical overturnings – the first shall be last, the poor are privileged, the uninvited are special guests – which make the kingdom of God look like Alice in Wonderland, like a divine topsy-turvy. The evangelists have Jesus announce his mission by way of a citation of Isaiah, that he brings good news to the poor, the hungry, the lame, and the imprisoned. Jesus' mission was to desperately poor people living from day to day, praying very literally for their "daily bread," the lowest social stratum in an occupied country in an obscure corner of a powerful empire, the very nobodies of this world Paul is describing.

II Icon of the Invisible God.

Jesus took the side of the oppressed and fearlessly spoke truth to the power of the Romans and the religious authorities. Still, Christians are not just saying that Jesus was a great man, a courageous truth-teller, and a martyr for the truth. We already have Socrates for that. The distinctly Christian claim is that apart from his human qualities, there is something qualitatively different about Jesus, which marks the qualitative difference between the human and divine. The Christian claim is that in Jesus we are given an *intuition of the divine* – that Jesus is an *icon* of the invisible God (Col 1:15). Socrates was an icon but of an entirely different sort. He incarnated the Greek principle, where the divine meant wisdom, power and being. He was an iconic man of reason, of the laws of the polis. Jesus is an icon of the prophetic principle, where the divine meant solidarity with the outlaws and the victims of the polis, which is the foolishness of God.

So if Christians are asked, "who do you say God is?" the answer has to be found not by Greek metaphysical speculation but by looking at Jesus, and if that is so, then we must be ready to be turned upside down:

Faced with an armed enemy, he tell us to lay down our sword.
Faced with hatred, he counsels love.
Faced with an offense, he tell us to forgive, up to and including the act of forgiveness that is issued from the cross.

The characteristic features of God fall systematically on the side of forgiveness, non-violence, and mercy, not of a sovereign lord and mighty conqueror. Unlike standard form heroes in antiquity, Jesus does not crush his enemies with his might but is instead defeated – arrested, tortured and subjected to a particularly cruel and, in an honour/shame society, humiliating public execution. The iconic body on the cross is itself one of the most abject of the *me onta*.

But this is governed by the paradoxical logic of reversals, where "the weakness of God is stronger than human strength" (1 Cor 1:25). The power of love, mercy, and forgiveness is greater than the power of brute force and merciless retaliation. So there is *power* here, but it is the *power of powerlessness*, a power *without force*. The divine realm is found in solidarity with everything that the world despises, where God mixes with the nothings and nobodies, pitching his tent among the shanty towns of the world. This divine realm contradicts the power of the "world" in the New Testament, where what holds sway is the clenched fist, the strong force of the power of the present age, the human-all-too human way of doing business, the authority of "man" over other men and women – and animals and the earth itself.

This throws the top down schema of one Sovereign God in heaven – "God of gods, King of kings, Father Almighty" – into reverse. The schema of the God of omnipotence who crushes his enemies succumbs to that of a more powerless power. The image of God in the classical theology of omnipotence derives from the Greek principle, and it is at odds with the icon of God imaged by Jesus, which derives from the prophets. This God is not lacking in strength, but the strength is located precisely *in the weakness*, in what the world calls weakness. So Paul – at least in 1 Cor 1 – is not denouncing power and strength but reimagining it according to the icon of the cross, relocating it according to the logos, the para-logic, of the cross. If Jesus is the distinctive and defining way that the invisible God is made visible to us, then the God that is thus revealed reverses our expectations: a God not of sovereign power but of *weakness*, a stunning reversal.

III The Church

Jesus, we should recall, is not the "founder" of "Christianity," of which he never heard. He was publicly executed long before he had a chance to found anything. If Christianity dares to take up his name, the name of this outsider and outcast, who represents the upside-down reversal of what the world expects, then it has a paradox on its hands. It is an institution, which means a worldly power, that exists in the name of a powerless power, a power which does not operate by way of worldly force. If the Christian presupposition is that "God" stands for an event that scandalizes the upper crusts of power, knowledge and privilege, then the institutions and structures of Christianity must be porous, open, bottom-up, hospitable, where justice reigns, not the institution. On that point the church is still a work in progress.

The paradox can be seen in the liturgical calendar where the feast of "Christ the King" is celebrated shortly before the season of advent, when the church prepares for the birth of a little baby under the humble circumstances described in the infancy narratives. This *child* – what the American womanist theologian Delores Williams calls "poor little Mary's boy"[1] – emblematizes for us *the divinity of true power*, the power of the truly divine. Then which is it? A child or a King? There is, of course, no paradox at all in a child born to become king, but the Christian paradox is that the royalty is lodged in the child as such, that is, the power is found in the weakness, not *in spite of* the weakness. This is a hard saying.

IV 1 Cor 2.

Too hard, I think, even for Paul, who did not adhere to his principle of weakness, folly and nullity with absolute rigour. In 1 Cor 2 he pretty much walks back what he said in 1 Cor 1, which now looks like a ruse. The tables are turned on the powers that be. They did not *recognize* the Lord Jesus and mistakenly cast their lot with Satan, and they will rue the day they did. They are doomed to perish, Paul says, when the *real power* of God will overthrow the powers of darkness and evil. I came to you in weakness, he says, but this weakness rests upon the power of God, by which he now means power as the world knows power. He does not mean the power of the kiss, of love, of forgiveness, but apocalyptic power, a real worldly reversal of fortunes in which the celestial power of God will strike down |the powers and the principalities. *Christus victor*. The worldly ones think they are smart, but they will be outsmarted by the ones who are perfected in the ways of God (*teleiois*, 1 Cor 2:6), by those who know better, who have the spirit, and know where the real power lies. So the first chapter is compromised by the second. Paul's idea, it turns out, is to overthrow human violence with divine violence, in which God almighty punishes the evil doers and rewards his saints handsomely. As Dale Martin says, "Ultimately, what Paul wants to oppose to human power is not weakness but divine power (2:5)—that is, power belonging to the other realm."[2]

V The Unconditional

But if not even the apostle Paul himself goes far enough with his vision of the weakness of God, how can such a weak God still be *God* at all? Where is God's true power? I approach the Godhead of God as something unconditional, of unconditional worth and importance. This I identify as an unconditional appeal or *call*, a claim that is *unconditional but without force or coercive power* to which we, who are on the other end of this call, respond unconditionally, without being subjected to coercive force.[3] The operative distinction for me is between the unconditional address contained in the name of God and our unconditional response. The name of God is the name of something that lays claim to us, that draws us out of ourselves and calls upon us, not from on high but from down below, from among the nothings and nobodies of the world. The unconditional requires us to respond to the call but without coercion, without a promise of worldly victory, without an economy of celestial rewards and punishments, "without why," as the Rhineland mystics say.

The call that issues from the hungry is without coercive force; the "world" is well-known for ignoring it. We are asked to respond to this call *unconditionally*, which means to feed the hungry because the hungry are hungry, without condition, without a promise or a threat. The kingdom of God is not a *reward* for feeding the hungry. Feeding the hungry is the kingdom of God, what it would be like if God ruled. The kingdom comes intermittently, every time the hungry are fed and the oppressed are lifted up, period, *simpliciter*. To think, to speak, to pray the coming of the kingdom of God is to imagine a *realm where the unconditional* holds sway, a realm of the unconditional, which is my candidate for a translation of the Greek.

I locate God's power in the powerless power of the call, where powerless implies it can always be rejected, ignored, scorned or distorted and, with any worldly luck, with complete impunity. The rich get richer and they get away with it. That is the *basileia* of the *world*, the way the power of the world works. Might makes right. I do not and cannot recognize any divinity at all in the power of a God who promises retaliation, who will make our enemies our footstool, who will come one day in apocalyptic power to reverse the fortunes of the downtrodden and crush the evildoers. The power of *that* God is worldly, not divine. The weakness of *that* God is a thinly disguised power play, a ruse pulled off on the worldly-wise who are not as smart as they think they are, which is what Nietzsche meant by the *resentment* of the religious soul. *That* God, as Paul Tillich says, is "half-blasphemous and mythological," and to that God the right religious and theological response is atheism.[4]

VI The Subjunctive Power of God

Rushing to a conclusion – I have defended all this elsewhere – this weakness must be applied to theology itself. The theology of the cross must also be a crucified theology.[5] The weakness of God must issue in a weak theology, one that is weakened into theo*poetics*.[6] The kingdom or rule of God is a *poem* to what the world would look like if God ruled, not the powers and principalities, and Jesus is its *poet*. The *basileia* has the power of a poem, the power of a dream, the power of a prayer. If we press the question of what such a world *would look like* – now the emphasis falls on the *would*, on the subjunctive – one answer is found in the poem to the realm of God in Isaiah, which the Church takes to be a pre-figuring of Jesus' kingdom:

> The wolf shall live with the lamb, the leopard shall lie down with the kid, the calf and the lion and the fatling together, and a little child shall lead them. (Isaiah 11:6)

The Subjunctive Power of God

This is not biological speculation. Neither is it a divine revelation of a coming turn in the history of evolution or in the course of human history. This is a poem, a prophetic song, and a prayer, a prophetic yearning. May this happen, please. May thy kingdom come. How long, O Lord? The power of being (*être*) lies in the may-being (*peut-être*); the might of God almighty lies in the might-be. The prophet Isaiah is a visionary, but he is not predicting a future event, like making a meteorological forecast. A prophecy is a poetic *vision* of a world in which a divine order prevails. The year of the Jubilee is coming but it is not found in calendar time. The "fiftieth" year is not a mathematical number; we keep counting but we never get to fifty. The kingdom of God is not a prediction of an age to arrive at some presently unknown date in the future. Neither is it to be found in another metaphysical world outside space and time, which is the Neoplatonic rendering – and I would say distortion – of the New Testament. The kingdom of God does not exist; it *insists*.[7] The kingdom of God does not exist; it calls. It is what is being dreamt of, prayed for, called for – come, *viens, oui, oui,* amen, *erchou*. The realm of God does not refer to a *different world* but to a poetic vision of how *this world* would be *different*, how it *would look*, in the subjunctive, if the powerless power of God held sway. The power of God is subjunctive.

I hasten to add that this powerless power is nothing anaemic and indecisive. The power of the subjunctive is not subjective. The power of the subjunctive is the power of a dream, not an idle dream, but a prophetic dream, like the dream of Martin Luther King, Jr. "I have a dream," he said, of a world in which "all of God's children" will be free. This is a dream for which King – his name is ironic – was not willing to take anyone else's life but he was willing to lay down his own life. That is how the subjunctive power of God works. That is how the kingdom comes.

Bibliography

J. D. Caputo, *Cross and Cosmos: A Theology of Difficult Glory*, Bloomington: Indiana University Press, 2019.

J. D. Caputo, *The Insistence of God: A Theology of Perhaps*, Bloomington: Indiana University Press, 2013.

J. D. Caputo, *The Weakness of God: A Theology of the Event*, Bloomington: Indiana University Press, 2006.

C. Chalamet/H.C. Askani (ed.), *The Wisdom and Foolishness of God: First Corinthians 1-2. In Theological Exploration*, Minneapolis: Fortress Press, 2015.

J. Derrida, *Without Alibi*, ed. and trans. Peggy Kamuf, Stanford: Stanford University Press, 2002.

D. B. Martin, *The Corinthian Body*, New Haven, CT: Yale University Press, 1995.

P. Tillich, *Theology of Culture*, ed. Robert C Kimball, Oxford: Oxford University Press, 1959.

D. Williams, "Rituals of Resistance in Womanist Worship," in M. Procter-Smith and J. R. Walton (ed), *Women at Worship: Interpretations of North American Diversity*, Louisville, KY: Westminster/J. Knox Press, 1993, 215-22.

Notes

1. D. Williams, "Rituals of Resistance in Womanist Worship," in M. Procter-Smith and J. R. Walton (ed), *Women at Worship: Interpretations of North American Diversity*, Louisville, KY: Westminster/J. Knox Press, 1993, 215-223: 216-217.
2. D. B. Martin, *The Corinthian Body*, New Haven, CT: Yale University Press, 1995, 62. See also C. Chalamet/H.C. Askani (ed.), *The Wisdom and Foolishness of God: First Corinthians 1-2. In Theological Exploration*, Minneapolis: Fortress Press, 2015.
3. Jacques Derrida analyzes the "unconditional without sovereignty" in J. Derrida, "The University without Condition," in *Without Alibi*, ed. and trans. Peggy Kamuf, Stanford: Stanford University Press, 2002, 202-37.
4. P. Tillich, *Theology of Culture*, Ed. Robert C Kimball, Oxford: Oxford University Press, 1959, 25.
5. J. D. Caputo, *Cross and Cosmos: A Theology of Difficult Glory*, Bloomington: Indiana University Press, 2019.
6. J. D. Caputo, *The Weakness of God: A Theology of the Event*, Bloomington: Indiana University Press, 2006. Spanish translation: *La Debilidad de Dios: una teleologia de acontecimiento*, Trans. Raúl Zegarra, Buenos Aires: Promoteo Libros, 2014; French translation: *La faiblesse de Dieu: Une Théologie de l'événement*, trans. John E. Jackson, Geneva: Labor et Fides, 2016.
7. J. D. Caputo, *The Insistence of God: A Theology of Perhaps*, Bloomington: Indiana University Press, 2013. French translation of chapters 2-3 in: John Caputo, "Faiblesse de Dieu et déconstruction de la théologie," ed. Elian Cuvillier, *Études Théologiques et Religieuses*, Volume 90 (No. 3): 2015.

The Inter-Action of Power and Authority: The Force of the Symbol and the Strengthening of Reality

JOÃO J. VILA-CHÃ

This paper aims at an articulation of authority and power as elements that are constitutive of the human condition. The question of power and authority is social and political, but also intrinsically theological. Therefore, the paper underlines the relational nature of both authority and power, analysis the dangers associated with its degradation, affirms its redeemability and, consequently, its inevitability for both Church and State. Our ultimate goal, however, is to assert how in order to be salvific, power and authority have to be limited, that is, structurally contained. While in the political society this happens in terms of a deep regard for the Constitution and the consequent Rule of Law, in the Church it remains inseparable from personal and faithful obedience to the incarnated Word of God.

Karl Barth explained the *power* of the Church as derived from "the Holy Spirit of Pentecost", the event that brought together the old prophetic word and the new apostolic one and so became effective witness of the Christ of God to many peoples and countless generations.[1] In and through the Spirit, the *Logos* of God reveals itself both in the spoken and in the written word and so becomes the *Word* through which the *power* of God becomes manifest across the world. Inasmuch as it is the Spirit of the Son, i.e., the Word of God made flesh, word spoken and written, the Spirit that speaks in the hearts of the believers is "the Spirit of the Prophets and of the Apostles".[2] Barth, therefore, posited as the ultimate source of power and authority in the Church the Spirit of the Word, that is, the One that guides the Church into the plenitude of truth.[3] Only in conjunction with Word and Spirit can we speak of authentic power and true authority in the Church. Power and authority are in the Church always *limited* and *contained*.[4]

In the Christian tradition, therefore, the ultimate source of power and authority is God the creator and redeemer. At the root of the Christian understanding of the human person is the principle that every human being is created in the image and likeness of God.[5] God endows the human person with the responsibility of achieving *dominion* over the world. That, however, must happen in *obedience* and through the constant recognition that in God alone reside supreme power and authority. As power and authority are constitutive parts of our being-in-the-world, they must always be exercised in terms of a relational act of God, that is, under the cover of a divine mandate. As gifts of God, power and authority demand to be understood in connection with His command.

In our self-understanding as creatures of God, we must recognize that power and authority are inseparable from our relationship with God, the One that transferred into human hands the capability of being/becoming *image* and *likeness* of the love which God is.[6] As creatures, the mandate received is to exercise dominion in the likeness of the one and eternal Ruler.[7] To deny God, therefore, would amount to the rejection of any ultimate foundation in our ethical paradigms, especially when it comes to the exercise of authority and power. Whenever it happens, both power and authority, as any other form of dominion, become open to forms of abuse and denial of human dignity. For the Christian person, therefore, the exercise of power and authority must never become unbridled or unlimited, exercised outside of rules and norms.[8] Power and authority have to be seen in relation with God and, consequently, be exercised in contemplation of the *kenotic* style of God, that is, of the One that rules and governs the world with infinite love and tenderness.

I The Meaning of Authority

Authority comes from the Latin *augeo*, a word that means things such as to make grow and to increase. The idea of development and growth, therefore, is originally implied in the semantic of the word authority. As it is natural for growth to be defined by its beginning and end, derivatives of *augeo* have been specified in both the sense of "to produce, to bring forth" and of "to perfect, to accomplish".[9] In this context, Gaston Fessard connects the noun *auctor* to the concept of growth and relates the word *auctoritas* – from which *authority* directly derives – to the kind of growth and development that in and for itself accomplishes things deserving of being considered as model and example for others. Cicero even designates the man of action as *auctor rerum* and uses *auctoritas* to affirm the value of whatever has been realized and can be taken as an example of something important.[10] The various meanings of *authority* reveal the presence of a dynamism that produces, grows and perfects the ontological bond that unites beings in their diversity and plurality. Fessard captures the essence of *authority* when he writes that the word means "the power that generates the social bond".[11] In the Fessardian sense, authority is not just the source of the *social* bond, but also the element that furthers its growth and brings about its ontological fulfilment.

In order to understand the meaning of *authority* we must learn to look at it as something that goes beyond the usual common sense of the legal power that constitutes the backbone and principle of unity of the State or any other institution incorporated under the rule of law. Rather, since authority is inseparable from growth and development, its exercise must be connected with the flourishing of the social being from which it depends. Even when concentrated in the hands of a prince, the uses of *authority* are inseparable from precise purposes and determined manners. Regardless of whoever has the capacity to exercise it, *authority* must always aim at the growth of the social body and the common good of its members.[12] If we look at the rule of law, for example, it becomes clear that the nature of *law* is permeated by the demand to serve *authority*, that is, to correspond to the *power* it is called to serve.

Strictly speaking, *power* always refers to a force, namely, to that force that independently of any right or reason, always affects others.[13] Power always grows in situations placed between the most brutal and the most ethereal. Hence the need, for example, to recognize the difference between the ascendant attained by the robber who, because of his exceptional vigour, cunning and brutality, becomes a successful gang leader, and that of the saint who, by his virtues and the radiance of his kindness, leads many to the achievement of ever greater good.[14] The point is that, regardless of its content being physical, psychic, intellectual or simply moral, *power* always constitutes a *force* associated with whoever is endowed with *authority*.[15]

II Degenerative Power

E. Mounier clarified how *authority* establishes *power* and, while remaining one of its foundations, finds in it the instrument it needs.[16] In line with the Christian personalism of the twentieth century, we can say that power owes its value and finds the law of its proper exercise in the presence of real *authority*. Every factual power, therefore, is grounded in a given authority. On the other hand, all authority finds expression in and through the exercise of power.[17]

As in all things human, there is always the danger that power, the natural instrument at the service of authority, degenerates into something different from its proper nature. In ancient Greece, the notion of *degeneration* appears inseparable from the good city, that is, from where human nature can best be implemented. According to Aristotle, the good city has characteristics such as legislative stability, implements adequate to the well-being of the citizens, excellent education.[18] A *polis* would then be good whenever it provides adequate education, is endowed with a sound constitution and, no less, enforces administrative measures that ensure the survival and the prosperity of all citizens. In this sense, the perversion of power happens whenever situations are created that diverge or contradict the purpose for which *power* was established.[19]

In *The Human Condition*, Hannah Arendt made clear that the exercise of power and the uses of violence are not the same. She writes: "Power is what keeps the public realm, the potential space of appearance between acting and speaking men, in existence. The word itself, its Greek equivalent *dynamis*, like the Latin *potentia* with its various modern derivates or the German *Macht* (which derives from *mögen* and *möglich*, not from *machen*), indicates its "potential" character. Power is always, as we would say, a power potential and not an unchangeable, measurable, and reliable entity like force or strength."[20] The implications of this passage are many, but here we just underline the fact that whenever violence emerges, *politics* is denied and that with the denial of the political the inevitable result is in every case the degradation of *power*. H. Arendt is also particularly illuminating in the attempt to understand the totalitarian phenomenon, especially Nazism and Stalinism.[21] Of special interest to us today, however, might be the consideration of the degrading nature of situations associated with the development of bureaucracies entirely divorced from the metaphysical force constituted by personal responsibility.[22]

Since the beginning of his papal ministry, Pope Francis never tires of reminding his listeners of the dangers caused by degenerative uses of power. Such is the case whenever the logic of the Spirit gives way to the vain aspirations of the human heart. Whoever holds power in a vain and superficial manner, normally, becomes addicted to holding it and, by necessity, never stops in yearning for more. Abuse, therefore, is always associated with a dynamic in which the person is overwhelmed by an insatiable yearning for power and by the search for more and more durable forms of power, for power less and less challenged and more and more disconnected from the real and concrete situations of human life. As a rule of thumb, "whoever, with vanity, aspires to power, always and in any case, first, loses concreteness and, second, becomes entangled in purely personal forms of self-incensement, instead of leading and carrying out his mission responsibly."[23] Vanity constitutes a psycho-social dynamic that frequently induces people, including in the Church, to either lack concreteness or entirely dismiss personal responsibility in the exercise of power. Pope Francis insists in a particular way upon the dangers of self-referentiality when in conjunction with the exercise of power. As such, self-referentiality implies the denial of truth as it induces the human subject, especially the one endowed with real power, to embrace self-centeredness, even to the risk of self-idolatry, as a way of life. In this, we might recognize one of the reasons why demagoguery and false populism constitute a major threat to democracy.

III Power Redeemed

The problem with power is that the human being is deeply affected by the experience of having it, at least when it happens above a certain measure. Whoever gains power always has problems remaining *ordinary*. By developing a sense of the measure of one's role, of one's technical abilities and of one's personal ethical values, a person can preserve *authenticity* in the exercise of authority and power. We need, thus, to permanently enter into the discerning process requested by the necessity of assuming that the person entrusted with the uses of power never stops being a person just like anyone else, and so remains constantly exposed to the dangers of abusing. Achieving authenticity in the exercises of power remains inseparable from a complex network of virtues, at the centre of which, perhaps, should be *humility*.[24]

Humility is a virtue well-spoken of in religious contexts. Yet the achievement of authenticity in the exercise of power is not a prerogative of Christians or believers in any other faith. It simply means that authenticity cannot be achieved in separation from the human cultivation of inferiority. Only "within oneself" is a person truly capable of deciding the extent to which he or she might cope with temptation. Thinkers of India such as Aurobindo or Gandhi, and Europeans such as Proudhon or Péguy have insisted upon the idea that the present conditions of any given society will never be adequately transformed until there is a betterment of the moral condition in its members. Social and political reform disconnected from the moral transformation of one's self is fallacious in nature. Karl Rahner would perhaps say that "the politician" of the future would have to be a *mystic* in order to bring about the changes needed. Giorgio La Pira, the former mayor of Florence, would certainly agree with the German theologian. Any attempt at the exercise of power in separation from a constant reference to higher principles, even if not necessarily religious, cannot but bring about corruption and the degeneration of such exercise.[25]

The issue here is how to understand *power* and *authority* in redemptive terms. First, we need to recognize the nature of power, namely, its *relational* constitution. Whoever is endowed with authority and power is in a *commanding* position and, thus, can exert influence upon others. Hence the dimension of *publicness* associated with power and authority, as Hannah Arendt so well demonstrated. In the understanding of the human condition, we can no longer separate the life of the self from our basic *Mit-sein*, being and living with others. To understand power, therefore, is to understand the extent to which we are related to one another.[26] The realization of power happens in the community. An authentic leader, thus, never answers for his actions to himself alone, but always places him- or herself in the presence of others.[27] To discern one's exercise of power and authority is, in each case, a matter of personal conscience. Yet it always depends on the communitarian or social context in which it actually happens.[28]

In order to redeem power and authority we need to reaffirm the relationship between the personal and the communitarian dimensions of human life. But we also must pay attention to the systemic workings of the institutions in and through which power and authority are exercised. A good institution is one that charters the different ways in which its members are called to exercise control and affirm the responsibilities that are part of it. A functioning democracy, for example, presupposes elections at regular times and under specific conditions. Needless to say, democracies are all the better the more they become capable of putting into action adequate systems of control and, even more, of enforcing their own ethical and moral substance. Political discernment, therefore, is inseparable from life in the community and always depends on the quality of the institutional parameters that surround it.[29]

No human power is self-sustaining since power and authority always depend on particular relationships, are sustained by them, and always remain at the service of them. Whenever the holders of power isolate themselves or become isolated, their power easily degenerates into corruption, despotism, if not violence and other major forms of self-destruction.[30] To achieve an authentic knowledge of power is, therefore, indispensable for both the exercise of power and the assessing process of whoever exercises it. In order to evaluate power one needs to have a "general education in relationality, here understood as the ability to know how to live consciously and responsibly in the family, at school and university, in the work environment and in the trade union, in a community of believers or in associative, administrative and different political contexts."[31] An assessment of power can only be fruitful if, once educated to the proper conditions of social and political life, we learn not just how to uncover systemic knowledge but also to distinguish among myriads of emotional states operating in the human soul.

IV State Power

A primordial prerogative of the State is the monopoly of punitive power. The State punishes in the measure that it has the power of coercion and so takes away from individuals the right to make justice for themselves. The incalculable value of the State derives from it being capable of containing the violence inherited from "man's primitive struggle against man" and until now scattered in human society.[32] When faced with violence, the individual can appeal to the State. But there is a danger, namely the one associated with the fact that the State frequently remains the last instance, i.e., the instance that does not allow for further recourse.[33] The centrality of the question regarding the authority and the power of the State remains crucial. Because of its multiple functions, "its power to legislate, its power to decide and execute, its administrative function, its economic function or its educational function," the State is endowed with the power to compel and to do so in last instance. After all, the power of the State is the power to coerce.[34]

Above we mentioned the danger of the wicked or totalitarian State. Now we just reaffirm "what makes the state a state, through different and even opposed regimes and forms."[35] That is, of course, the exercise of authority and power. Hence the gravity of situations in which the State becomes illegitimate and degrades itself into forms of abuse in the exercise of what should be its own authority and power. More than anything else, this is the reason why human societies are always in need of a strong conjunction of *law* and *force*. And the recognition that no State can "fully express, fully realize, radically exhaust all the requirements of moral conscience".[36] In other words, politics and the State must be taken for what they are, namely, as utterly incapable of achieving morality and fulfillment of all ethical demands constitutive of the human condition as such. No politics, and thus no State, can be said to be capable of ultimately quenching the human thirst for perfection.[37]

V Conclusion

To conclude, let's return once again to the thought of Gaston Fessard, and this not because the French Jesuit has rightly been identified as one of the most important influences in the formative process of Pope Francis,[38] but rather because according to Fessard, any attempt to grasp the essence of power and authority necessarily leads us to represent it on the one hand as "the continuous growth of a principle towards its end", and on the other "as two opposite movements between the poles of the individual and the universal."[39] Is this a sign of contradiction? I would say no, at least inasmuch as that double aspect of the political realm testifies to what for Fessard corresponds to the "rightness of the reflection" (*rectitude de la réflexion*). As an interpreter of both Hegel and the Spiritual Exercises of Saint Ignatius of Loyola,[40] Gaston Fessard knows that the duality of *power* and *authority* constitutes a symbol of the "circle whose movement, during a period of continuous growth, first unfolds between two diametrically opposed points, then withdraws into itself to rediscover, by an about turn, its principle in its end".[41]

Power and authority are symbolic of the *search* that both philosophy and theology represent and of the political life that sustain our societies in their historical processes. In seeking to understand the nature and essence of both *authority* and *power*, we realize that power is *procreative*, as represented in the figure of the *father*; that the Hegelian dialectic of Master-Slave expresses the structure and the dynamic of domination and its transformation in accordance with the logic of freedom; that Man-Woman and the consequent constitution of the family opens the door to the primacy of the Common Good and the ineluctable transformation of individual effort into the universality of the Kingdom.

Notes

1. Cf. Karl Barth, *Vorträge und kleinere Arbeiten*, 1922-1925, ed. Holger Finze, Digital Karl Barth library (Zürich: Theologischer Verlag, 1990), p. 664.
2. Ibidem.
3. Cf. Jn 16:13.
4. Karl Barth, op. cit..
5. Cf. Wolfhart Pannenberg, *Was ist der Mensch? Die Anthropologie der Gegenwart im Lichte der Theologie.*, 4., Aufl., Kleine Vandenhoeck-Reihe (Göttingen: Vandenhoeck & Ruprecht, 1972).
6. Cf. Gen. 1.
7. Cf. Rocco D'Ambrosio, *Il potere e chi lo detiene* (Bologna: EDB, 2008), p. 19.
8. Cf. Ibidem.
9. Cf. Gaston Fessard, *Autorité et Bien Commun*, 2. éd. augm. d'une postface (Paris: Aubier-Montaigne, 1969), p. 12.

10. Cf. Ibidem, p. 13.
11. Ibidem, p. 13 : «la puissance génératrice du lien social, tendant de soi à croître jusqu'à son accomplissement.»
12. Cf. Ibidem, p. 14.
13. Cf. Ibidem, pp. 14-15.
14. Cf. Ibidem, p. 15.
15. Cf. Ibidem.
16. Emmanuel Mounier, "Le destin spirituel du mouvement ouvrier: Anarchie et personnalisme," *Esprit* 5, no. 55 (1937), p. 109 f.
17. Cf. Rocco D'Ambrosio, *Il potere e chi lo detiene* (Bologna: EDB, 2008), pp. 16-17.
18. Cf. Ibidem, pp. 58-59.
19. Ibidem, p. 59.
20. Hannah Arendt, *The Human Condition*, Charles R. Walgreen Foundation Lectures (Chicago: University of Chicago Press, 1958), p. 200.
21. Cf. Hannah Arendt, *The Origins of Totalitarianism*, New ed., A Harvest Book (New York: Harcourt Brace Jovanovich, 1973).
22. Cf. Emmanuel Lévinas, Autrement qu'être; ou, Au-delà de l'essence, *Phaenomenologica* 54 (La Haye: MNijhoff, 1974).
23. Rocco D'Ambrosio, op.cit., p. 114.
24. Cf. Ibidem, p. 134.
25. Cf. Ibidem, p. 135.
26. Cf. Wolfhart Pannenberg, *Was ist der Mensch?*, pp. 60-61.
27. D'Ambosio, op.cit., p. 138.
28. On political discernment, see, for ex., João B. Libânio, *Spiritual Discernment and Politics: Guidelines for Religious Communities* (Maryknoll, NY: Orbis Books, 1982); Id., *Fé e política: autonomias específicas e articulações mútuas*, Coleção "Fé e realidade" 17 (São Paulo: Edições Loyola, 1985).
29. Cf. D'Ambosio, op.cit., p. 138.
30. Cf. Ibidem, p. 171.
31. Ibidem.
32. Cf. Paul Ricoeur, "La question du pouvoir," in *Histoire et vérité*, 3e éd. augmentée de quelques textes, Collection Esprit (Paris: Seuil, 1955), 235–316, p. 246 f.
33. Cf. Ibidem, p. 246.
34. Cf. Ibidem.
35. Cf. Ibidem, pp. 246-247.
36. Cf. Ibidem, p. 247.
37. Cf. Ibid.
38. Cf. Massimo Borghesi, *The Mind of Pope Francis: Jorge Mario Bergoglio's Intellectual Journey*, trans. Barry Huddock (Collegeville, Minnesota: Liturgical Press, 2018).
39. G. Fessard, op.cit., p. 32.
40. Cf. Gaston Fessard, La dialectique des Exercices spirituels de saint Ignace de Loyola, *Théologie* 35, 66 (Paris: Aubier, 1956).
41. Cf. Gaston Fessard, Autorité et Bien Commun, op.cit., p. 32.

Power As Service:
A Critical Reading of Power
from the New Testament

IVONI RICHTER REIMER & HAROLDO REIMER

Power is understood as a set of power relationships. We seek to highlight that within the context of these relations in the Roman empire in the first century, the texts of the New Testament mostly present the perspective of a counter-power or heterotopy. This is expressed through the concept and experience of the Kingdom of God. In a set of texts that presuppose and critically analyse the dominant power, the exercise of power is presented as diakonia, especially in relation to the most vulnerable people. Jesus is the model for this service-power, which empowers men and women in ekklēsíai to follow the Lord in faithfulness.

In the context of Latin America, there is an ambivalence in the relationship between Christian people and the exercise of power, between theology and politics. On the one hand, there remains a commitment to the preferential option for the poor, as expressed by Liberation Theology, carried out through public policies and non-governmental organizations. However, along the path of (re)structuring power relations, there was a process of co-optation or participation in post-liberal governments, which contributed to weakening the critical reserve in social and ecclesial movements. As social conditions and public policies, such as poverty and women's rights, have been partially addressed, new demands have been established. In this context, conservative fundamentalist and neo-Pentecostal Christian religious proposals have gained ground: religious groups and churches create, finance, and organize right-wing political parties, explicitly engaging in election campaigns, maintaining powerful and well-organized lobbies in Parliament; they share positions of power at local and national levels, utilizing strategies with international repercussions to occupy, in the medium and long term, positions and functions in the state apparatus. As these groups are structured around centralized and authoritarian forms of governance, the dimension of support for authoritarian and elitist governments gains space at an accelerated pace. Neo-Pentecostal and fundamentalist theologies are designed to support these new alliances in the field of politics, losing the critical dimension of theology.[1]

We believe that power does not exist as an abstract and fixed entity.[2] There are power relations, which are constantly built on variable transformations, serving as mechanisms for the effective exercise of power, which is manifested by physical, moral, psychological, ideological and religious coercion, disciplining individuals and collectivities. Not being an abstract entity, power is not located only in institutions such as the State/Church, but it is organized within a logic of 'microphysics of power', in which diverse interests can be brought to the plane or realization in a set of real and symbolic exchanges. Power, therefore, is a social practice that is structured in socio-cultural relations, always open to new constellations and constructions, according to the demands of the interested placed at stake in the respective correlation of forces. Thus, the concept of power is shifted from the centre to the extremities and to the mechanisms, through which power is effectively exercised, covering the various fields of social relations. The management of an ideological, warlike, bureaucratic, symbolic, and religious apparatus operates in such a way that individuals and collectivities adhere to it or oppose it, shape themselves or submit to these relationships, with different degrees of coercion or even with deliberate participation, depending on meeting personal or collective interests. Every socio-cultural structure, therefore, is permeated by such relationships and marked by conflicts.

In New Testament times, the dominant power structure was that of the Roman empire. In the 2nd century BC, Rome implemented expansion processes to occupy territorial spaces around the Mediterranean, which aimed at controlling the wealth produced and the subjugated bodies. The *imperium* as an exercise of power, control, and disciplining of different collectivities, within the project of the *pax romana*, which extended to the

3rd century, presupposes a set of structures and relations that must support this authoritarian greatness.[3]

Regarding the structure of the Roman empire, it can be said that the 'Roman peace' was solidified by the thriving military structure. With repeated conquests permeated by bravery and violence, by strategies and the wide exercise of subjugation and death of people and collectivities, the Roman army as the operational arm of centralized power managed to expand borders, guarantee dominance in a controlled space, impose Roman law and order, inhibiting and repressing resistance to this power. Various ancient Roman authors expressed support for this form of exercise of power, including ideologically granting divine dimensions to the emperor to reinforce his symbolic effectiveness.[4] With the use of military forces and recruited populations, it was possible to build a transport and communication system between the centre and the periphery, overcoming the natural obstacles of rivers, mountains, and swamps.[5] In addition to the control of ports, the Roman roads also established the conditions for the displacement of military contingents and goods to provide the Roman order and supply the capital's demands with agility. In order to maintain an administrative system in place that would allow for a relative degree of integration of the political and social forces of the dominated areas within the imperial structure, "Rome knew how to establish a community of interest between itself and the autochthonous upper classes",[6] thus evidencing degrees of adhesion and participation of the "margins' in the exercise of centralized power.

The ambiguous relationship of groups in the New Testament with such a structure of the consolidation of Roman power is reflected in the very use of the means of transport by roads and seas, built for the benefit of Rome: the Christian mission used these means of communication and transit to announce the Gospel, whose foundation constituted another type of government under the power of the *kyrios* Jesus of Nazareth, the Jewish messiah-king, whose peace was not 'of this world', but aimed at justice and the salvation of all people, especially those suffering the most. This counter-power was constituted from and for the benefit of the periphery.

Power relations established at the macro-level had a strong social component in terms of standardizing social relations. Roman ideologists cultivated the notion of patriarchy as the form of dominant relationship at the level of state organization and its projection especially in the 'home' as a micro-universe. Cicero developed the architecture and structure of a patrikyriarchal system for the government of the State and the House – two institutions that sustain each other- which presupposes and consolidates dualisms involving the relations of class, ethnicity, gender, and age.[7] With an elitist and androcentric perspective, man was determined to be the head of the extended family and this made it possible to give the State long-term support and stability, creating a cognitive and imaginary model far beyond that time. This projection and struggle for the maintenance of the patriarchal house also appears in the New Testament, in parallel with texts that question them (Galatians 3:26-28; Colossians 3: 18-4:1).

The texts of the New Testament reflect the conditions, structures and power relations in the Roman empire. Although the Gospels, which in their narratives combine historical and mythical elements,[8] refer to the early times of the Roman empire, under the emperors Augustus (27 BCE to 14 CE) and Tiberius (14-37 CE), the historical appearance of these texts comes from the period after the bloody government of Nero (54-68 CE) and especially during the period of the Flavian dynasty (Vespasian: 69-79 CE; Titus: 79-81 CE; and Domitian: 81-96 CE). The reflective dimension of the New Testament texts, in historical and theological terms, already presupposes incrimination and persecution of Christian people, especially under Nero, but also the destruction of Jerusalem and its consequences, under Vespasian and Titus.[9] Matthew 10: 16-42; John 16; Acts 1:8; 2:42-47; 4:32-35; 1 Corinthians 1:10-2:5, etc., are found in this context as a challenge and encouragement for resilience/ perseverance in the faith.

Looking at the whole, it can be said that most of these texts project something like a counter-power or a heterotopy, but in them there is no univocal position on the theme of power or exercise of power. It can be said that, in extreme terms, they oscillate between considering the embodiment of power in the Roman empire as 'The Beast' (Revelations 13), or considering the power structure as something instituted by God (Romans 13:1-7). Among these positions, however, there is a strong witness to the dimension of the exercise of power as a service/diakonia, highlighting the Kingdom of God as a counter-system in opposition to 'this world' governed by other principles. In this sense, John expresses the "world" (cosmos) as a political and socio-cultural structure in opposition to the Kingdom of God: believing people live under the conditions of 'this world', but do not belong to it as they are sons and daughters of God.[10] The Kingdom of God project includes the power relations of love, sharing, service, and communion, which are manifestations of faith in God, evidenced in the daily life of small Christian communities and which do not agree with relations of violence in any system.

In the synoptic Gospels, the critical discussion of power also focuses on the affirmation of Jesus as the son of David. A set of passages places Jesus in the line of David, therefore, in the claim to exercise real power in the context of that peripheral world in the Roman empire. The triumphal entry of Jesus into Jerusalem (Mark 11; 14 and parallels), in the events prior to the Passion on the occasion of Easter, highlights this trait. However, the narrative itself distances itself from the representations of such acts by other rulers, by reference to the donkey instead of the horse, as well as the simple popular procession instead of the royal pomp. In the evangelical representation, the contours of the Davidic ruler assume the popular traits, of people who lend a space to hold the Easter supper, because they have no property. These traits correspond to Jesus' projection as Lord who rules with simplicity.

One of Jesus' most significant words about the exercise of this counter-power, which is power in relationship and power-service, is found in Mark 10:42-45 (Matthew 20:25-28; Luke 22: 25-26): the greatest is the one that serves, indicating clearly by this the inversion of values consolidated by patriarchal ideologies. This is a critical heritage that is rarely lived out in the history of the Church. In it, Jesus refers to the exercise of political power of his time and, if we look closely, Mark 10:42 explicitly denounces the relations of this power. Unlike Luke and Matthew, he does not use affirmatively the term "kings" or "rulers" and much less does he honour them for being called *euerguétai* "benefactors". On the contrary, between criticism and irony, he says: "those who think about (*dokéō*) governing peoples...". Those who think about ruling, use the coercive manorial force of submission (*katakyriéuō*). The preposition *katá*, in the verb composed in Mark and Matthew, qualitatively differentiates the exercise of political power "over" dominated peoples, while Luke uses the simple verb *kyriéuō* "to dominate", which harmonizes power relations and minimizes coercive force. The same occurs with the verb *exousiázō* (Luke 22:25), which expresses an exercise of power, while Mark 10:42 and Matthew 20:25 use *katexousiázō*, indicating greater coercion in this exercise. Taking the example of the government of the people, in this case the macrostructure of the Roman empire, the denial of this form of government and the rejection of this model of the exercise of power is clear and evident in the three gospels: "But it is not so with you!" Jesus takes enslaved people (*diáconos* and *doulos*) as a model of governance in the service of the Kingdom of God and with this theologically dismantles the imperial power structure. In Mark and Matthew, the argument for such an inversion in the exercise of power is the praxis of Jesus himself, now confessed Son of Man by the *ekklēsíai*-communities: He did not come to be served but to serve and to give his life. We have a significant difference here as compared to Romans 13:4, where the authority is also considered to be *diáconos* of God amid dualistic relations of good-evil power, as an instrument of punishment and revenge: one executes. Here, on the contrary, Jesus is a *diáconos* who gives his life!

Microstructures of power within the larger structure of the imperial system also deserve attention, such as power relations in religions, corporations, and homes. Here there are movements of alliance, but also armed and non-armed resistance, like the movement of John the Baptist and Jesus.[11] Both had a prophetic and eschatological character, experiencing adherence and rejection. John the Baptist had Jesus as a follower, opening paths for him to act, which were expanded in various ways demonstrating the liberating power of Jesus, questioning any exercise of power that creates oppression, suffering, discrimination, subjugation, and exclusion. According to New Testament narratives, it can be stated that:

a) Jesus healed women and men of any age, ethnicity, gender and class, mainly impoverished. With this, he strengthened popular therapeutic movements and the search for alternative paths through faith, placing its characteristics of compassion, gratuity, and power-service. Thus, he questioned the enrichment of doctors at the expense of sick people, religious traditions and practices of purity and impurity, manifestations of discrimination and marginalization by people and collectives and the political-economic domain that enslaves people to the point of making them the living-dead.[12] The exercise of this power is relational and therapeutic, aiming at health and salvation;

b) Jesus welcomed people considered unworthy, incapable and marginalized: women, children, slaves, day labourers, artisans, employees, and shared knowledge, care, love, food and drink with them, announcing the Good News in villages and cities, on roads, houses, synagogues, in the temple and on the beaches. He was humble and energetic, had words of comfort and denunciation, faced tribulations and admitted fatigue and loneliness, cried, laughed and allowed himself to be touched by women and men. This praxis of his resulted in discipleship of people equal in the love and liberating mercy of God, and with this he questioned the power relations that segregate, elitize, disqualify, reject and violate through mechanisms of submission, exploitation, and occupation;

c) Jesus taught based on his knowledge of the Torah, history, traditions, and popular wisdom and was able and open to doing this with humble people through sermons, sayings and parables and with doctors through disputes that presupposed hermeneutical- exegetical management equal to that of his colleagues. With this, he questioned the closure and the elitization of knowledge, placing it at the service of life and the Kingdom of God and criticizing institutions that do it to maintain status. It is in this sense that he affirmed, for example, that the Sabbath is at the service of human beings, and not the other way around!

d) Jesus had, in some houses, his base of work and existence. In them, women also exercised management, care, and leadership functions. The house of Jesus and for Jesus is a space of life, welcome, respect, equality, healing and solidarity. For him, family0home is not based on patriarchal structures, but on carrying out God's will. The 'base cell' is not the patriarchal home of Roman state ideology, but the brotherhood in the service of the Kingdom of God (see item f).

e) John the Baptist died beheaded and Jesus hung on the cross. In their praxis, both were rejected, denounced, condemned and executed by those who lived power relations "over", for the benefit of political and religious systems of domination, control, and occupation. However, torture and the cross became a representation of the denunciation of powers exercised with violence and injustice, as well as symbolic of the precariousness and fragility of human judgments. The memory of John the Baptist in the Jesus movement honours religious activities that stand as mediators of conflicts and precursors of peace. The memory of Jesus's resurrection fosters hope of freedom/liberation, questioning every exercise of power that subordinates, tortures, and kills. Women were the first witnesses of this resurrection, and this testimony calls for power relations that are placed at the service of injured life, also today and especially of the thousands of women who are raped and killed daily!

f) This liberating praxis of Jesus was reinvented in multiple and different experiences of rebuilding life-in-following after Jesus after his death and resurrection, as also expressed in letters and Acts of the Apostles. Jesus' conception of the family home became so important that the homes of women and men became *ekklēsíai* of freedom/liberation, cells of resistance to Roman patriarchal structures.[13] Alongside the synagogues, houses became a space for the celebration of faith and the organization of community life. Insofar as they lived under the criteria of the Kingdom of God and its justice, they distanced themselves from the dynamics of current power relations, becoming spaces for the experimentation of counter-power. This was also expressed through the exercise of women's leadership, represented by Mary, Martha, Priscilla, Tabitha, Chloe, Phoebe, Junia, and many others. Paradoxically, however, some houses also became the reproductive axis of the patrikyriarchal ideology, as members of the non-Jewish elite began to convert to the Christian faith and this is still the 'Christian ideology' most widely proclaimed around the world today (see the domestic codes).

In conclusion: New Testament narratives pursue a communicative objective. The texts are addressed to original Christian communities that were in their structuring phase and also dealt with the administration of power relations within the *ekklēsíai*. Aims to exercise power in the manner of power relations in the Roman empire are contrasted with the exercise of service/diakonia, and this power-service was directed to the people most in need and made vulnerable by the system of *pax romana* system and by religious institutions that maintained status and power over people and their faith. People and churches today are called upon by the Lord of the Church to reinvent this critical heritage!

Translated by Thia Cooper

Notes

1. We recommend the reading of *Caminos, Special Issue: Religion and Politics*, Goiânia, v. 17/4 (2019), http://seer.pucgoias.edu.br/index.php/caminhos/issue/view/346 [accessed 17 December 2019].
2. See Michel Foucault, *Microfísica do poder*, Rio de Janeiro: Edições Graal, 1979.
3. We have as a reference for the consolidation of the structural aspects necessary for the exercise of such power, the elaboration of Thomas J. Barfield, "The shadow empires: imperial state formation along the Chinese-Nomad frontier", in Susan E. Alcock / Terence N. D´Altroy / Kathleen D. Morrison / Carla M. Sinopoli (Orgs.), *Empires: Perspectives from Archaeology and History*, Cambridge: Cambridge University Press, 2001, 130-146: a) an administrative system capable of exploring diversity; b) a transportation system to serve the imperial center; c) a communication system that allows all the subjugated áreas to be managed from the center; d) a military force capable of securing borders; e) the existence of an imperial Project that aims to create relative unity in the midst of diversity. All of these aspects are present in the Roman imperial system and were known in the New Testament context.
4. For this, see Klaus Wengst, *Pax romana. Pretensão e realidade* [*Pax Romana and the Peace of Jesus Christ*]. São Paulo: Paulinas, 1991. For divinization processes and relations between Politics and Religion, see Ivoni Richter Reimer / Danilo D. Guerra, Eliézer C. de Oliveira, "Ave César: a deificação do imperador como teatro de poder no império romano", *Plura – Revista de Estudos da Religião* 7/2 (2016), 78-93.
5. Narrativa de Tácito acerca das guerras de ocupação, seus resultados e recrutamento de jovens prisioneiros para essas construções: Ivoni Richter Reimer, *Economia no Mundo Bíblico: enfoques sociais, históricos e teológicos*, São Leopoldo: Sinodal; CEBI, 2006, 72-97.
6. Klaus Wengst, *Pax romana. Pretensão e realidade*, São Paulo: Paulinas, 1991, 42.
7. In this regard, see Ivoni Richter Reimer, *Economia no Mundo Bíblico: enfoques sociais, históricos e teológicos*, São Leopoldo: Sinodal; CEBI, 2006, 72-97; Luise Schottroff, *Befreiungserfahrungen: Studien zur Sozialgeschichte des Neuen Testaments*, München: Chr.Kaiser Verlag, 1989; Elisabeth Schüssler Fiorenza, *Caminhos da Sabedoria: uma Introdução à Interpretação Bíblica Feminista*, São Bernardo do Campo: Nhanduti Editora, 2009.
8. See Wolfgang Stegemann, *Jesus e seu tempo,* São Leopoldo: Sinodal; EST, 2012.
9. We rely here on the work of Wolfgang Stegemann, *Jesus e seu tempo*. São Leopoldo: Sinodal; EST, 2012; Klaus Wengst, *Pax romana. Pretensão e realidade*, São Paulo: Paulinas, 1991; Richard A. Horsley, *Jesus e o Império: o reino de Deus e a nova desordem*

mundial [*Jesus and Empire: The Kingdom of God and the New World Disorder*], São Paulo: Paulus, 2004.
10. See Johan Konings, *Evangelho segundo João: amor e fidelidade*, São Paulo: Loyola, 2005.
11. About the movements, see Richard A. Horsley, *Jesus e o Império: o reino de Deus e a nova desordem mundial*, São Paulo: Paulus, 2004; Wolfgang Stegemann, *Jesus e seu tempo*, São Leopoldo: Sinodal; EST, 2012.
12. This was the case for people with mental health problems and skin diseases. On the realities of disease and healing in antiquity see Ivoni Richter Reimer, *Milagre das Mãos: curas e exorcismos de Jesus em seu contexto histórico-cultural*, São Leopoldo: Oikos; Goiânia: Ed. da UCG, 2008.
13. Read Marlene Crüsemann / Ivoni Richter Reimer, "Igrejas Domésticas: Lugar de Acolhida, Partilha e Celebração na Casa de Mulheres", *Caminhos* 14/1 (2016), 179-190, http://seer.pucgoias.edu.br/index.php/caminhos/article/view/4835/2701 [accessed 17 December 2019].

Empowerment of the Disempowered: Some Glimpses into Jesus' Life and Mission

A. MARIA ARUL RAJA

The power accumulation by the socio-cultural hegemony of the ruling elite is to be encountered with valiant defiance through getting awakened to the God-given dignity in solidarity with other victims. The inner powers of the religio-cultural assertion of disempowered are to be consolidated through appropriate identification and interpretation of the symbols like the 'Reign of God' and the Cross. The uncompromising criterion of protecting and promoting life has to encounter the systemic politico-cultural violence.

The ethics of egalitarianism, the aesthetics of solidarity and empowerment with humanization seem to constitute the core of the power discourse of the life and mission of Jesus.

I Power Discourse in Jesus' Praxis

The contemporary chaos created by the profit-triggered culture of unbridled consumerism and violent developmentalism has to be encountered with an alternative vision and committed mission at the global level. The growing culture of hatred towards the people counted to be migrants and untouchables is to be replaced with the compassionate embrace of such marginalized people across various countries. When these disempowered people are further crushed down with multiple systemic evils, we need to identify alternate visions of their empowerment. This exploration into subaltern empowerment could be fruitful through a close re-reading of the power discourse transpired in the life and mission of Jesus. Perhaps, this could inspire the marginalized people for effectively envisioning a new world order free from every trace of discriminatory hierarchy.

This article seeks to identify some glimpses into the features of the politically sensitized theology set afloat by Jesus in the public space of his time i.e., the first century Palestinian soil of the Mediterranean world colonized by the Romans. Through the praxis of Jesus of Nazareth as transpired through the gospels one could surmise that he had been valiantly struggling against dehumanizing power-mongers in view of ushering in a new order of equals. Here we seek to spell out the following paradigms of the power discourse of Jesus.
- Defiance of Socio-cultural Hegemony
- Exploration into Religio-cultural Assertion
- Encountering Politico-cultural Violence

II Defiance of Socio-cultural Hegemony

Jesus seemed to have realized his mission as that of overcoming the evil powers which ruled the world to reinstate the ownership of the life-affirming divine.[1] The mighty deeds performed by Jesus in the Synoptic gospels are the interventions of delivering the suffering members of the *ochlos* from the clutches of evil powers (Mk 1:21-28; 40-45; 2:1-12; 5:1-42). Jesus' interventions labelled as miracles are the stories of healing from psycho-somatic disabilities, emancipation from psycho-spiritual possession, or liberation from religio-cultural prejudices. These actions are indicative of beginning of the new era of the oncoming God's reign through binding the Strong Man (the Evil One). The strongman and his army of evil spirits are noted with the use of "us" (Mk 1:24) and "Legion" and "many" (Mk 5:9).

The evocative powers of the parables, narrations, and stories of Jesus seemed to have at once created optimistic vibrations amidst the marginalized and infuriated resistance among the socio-cultural elite (Mt 21:28-32; Mk 2:1-12; 12:1-12; Lk 18:9-14). When his own native authorities were bent on terminating his life with the allegation of transgression of law even at the beginning of his mission (Mk 3:6), Jesus continued his acts of solidarity with the marginalized (Mk 2: 18-28). This trend of penalizing him also continued in his last days, but the authorities were afraid of doing so in the broad day light due to the massive support to Jesus from the simple folk (Mk 11:32; 12:12; 14:2). When questioned about his origin of his authority for doing all people-centred empowerment activities, his immediate and spontaneous reference to the baptism of John the Baptist (Mk 11:30) directly or indirectly alludes to his authority of being missioned as the Son of God (Mk 1:11).[2]

It is with this charismatic authority, he went ahead with the proclamation of the good news of the eruption of the reign of God through healing the sick and driving away the evils. The same authority for healing and exorcism was vested with his disciples (Mk 3:14-15). In the controversy stories both in Galilea (Mk 2:1-3:6) and Jerusalem (Mk 11:27-12:37), and also in the stories of criticism of the Temple (Mk 11:15-17, 27; 12:41-44; 13:1-3; 14:58; 15:29, 38), the political matrix of Jesus seems to converge on this orientation: 'Never become a slave and never enslave others'.

Interestingly, the self-designation of Markan Jesus as the son of Man has the following triple layers of implications:

• The power to courageously go beyond the traditions for protecting and promoting the welfare of the marginalized for upholding their human dignity is deployed by the Son of Man (Mk 2:10, 28).

• The power to valiantly encounter the violent consequences of such violations of the traditions is of such 'violations' is manifest in his mission (Mk 8:31; 9:31; 10:33-34).

• The power to be elevated by the divine glory after defeating the anti-human and anti-life forces (Mk 9:9; 14:62).

Here one could have some glimpses into the sequential order of the power dynamics operative in the life and mission of Jesus. Accordingly, his power as the Son of Man seems to have attained the divine glory as the result of his courageous encounter with suffering imposed by the ruling elite for his committed solidarity with the suffering masses of people. And obviously Jesus never hesitated to denounce those obsessed with power-accumulation in the following manner:

• Those seeking to lord it over others were counted as gentiles by him (Mk 10:42).

• Those preaching others with authoritative eloquence in public realm while never practicing the same in private realm are dismissed as the accursed ones (Mt 23:1-12).

• Those self-pontificating puritans setting a convenient yardstick for

themselves while setting another one for the same act were condemned (Mt 23:13-36).
• The native feudal power-brokers indiscriminately surrendering the hard-earned resources by the sweat of the labour class people at the feet of the alien colonial powers (symbolized by vultures seeking corpses - Mt 24:27-28) just for maintaining their own power positions like Herod (symbolized by foxes- Lk 13:32) were denounced.

This is how the prevailing culture of socio-cultural hegemony of the ruling elite was defied by the counter-cultural praxis undertaken by Jesus in solidarity with the large majority of the common folk excluded as sinners by the power-accumulators.

III Exploration into Alternative Religio-cultural Assertion

The militarized Roman colonial power of Jesus' time, in collaboration with the domesticated Palestinian religio-cultural elite, trampled upon all indigenous economic resources and communitarian ethos of the common people in the name of promoting Pax Romana. Both the alien and native ruling class were highly insensitive to the cultural sensibilities and popular religiosities prevalent among the marginalized (*ptōchoi* and *ochlos*). On the other hand, the radicals, advocating vehement protest against the colonizers, took to armed confrontation against Roman forces resulting in recurring blood-shed of the masses with the repression of the military intervention of the rulers.

Against this wounded historical scenario, Jesus, the committed rebel, proclaimed the reality of the outburst of the compassionate justice of the divine order, called the 'kingdom of God'.[3] It was said to be dwelling in the hearts of the ordinary folk as a grace-filled reality of the given past ('Time is fulfilled...kingdom of God has come near'- Mk 1:15) embedded in the present context ('is among you'- Lk 17:21) with gradual blossoming forth in future ('your kingdom come'- Mt 6:10). This sense of hope and happiness, though snatched away from the least by the evil powers, should be recuperated. Such was the fundamental orientation of the reign of the living God as envisaged by Jesus with the following movement on the historical plane here and now:

Whenever this concrete life-affirming movement took place, Jesus

Movement From	Movement Towards
From the brokenness of the Body, Mind, Spirit, Life and Cosmos crushed unto Death	Towards becoming activated by the life-giving spirit of the Living God

celebrated it exuberantly. It is with this life-generating spirit and life-promoting determination that God is living and reigning was his irrefutable conviction.

Jesus never converted the reality of the 'reign of God' into an intricate ideology to be debated, an elaborate constitution to be discussed, or a meta-narrative to be recounted. He did not give his life for an ideology, constitution, or meta-narrative. Rather he garnered all his energies to enable the marginalized people to claim their rightful place in the world at once wounded and wounding. In all his matter-of-fact interventions, labelled as mighty deeds, grand signs, or he minutely identified that the 'reign of God' gradually sprouting and blossoming forth. He expected that these gradual and continual movements of promoting the culture of life has to be experienced as the unconditional love of God both at individual and collective levels. The positive strokes like 'stretch out your hand' (Mk 3:5), 'your faith has made you well' (Lk 17:19), or 'get up and walk' (Jn 5:8) were the hall marks for enlivening those who were groomed in the culture of self-hatred. The people like the Samaritans, women, and differently abled, chronically sick or dying destitutes counted as irretrievably polluted untouchables were affirmed with motherly care and fatherly compassion as a full-fledged member of Jesus' community.

Jesus did not project the 'reign of God' sprouting and yielding as the performance of a super star. Each of his socio-political and religio-cultural intervention in the broken world of his times eventually was made to be communitarian task, be it healing or exorcism, washing of the feet, egalitarian sharing of breaking, or good-news-ing the nations. The political alliance required for his praxis, Jesus seemed to have carefully and perceptively chosen with appropriate discernment. He did not join hands with any of the following groups as his partners for his collective socio-political and religio-cultural interventions:

1. Dominating Powers: The imperial Roman colonizers, Herod the fox
2. Opportunist Powers : The self-righteous and profit-oriented persons
3. Weaponry Powers: The underground groups advocating attacks with arms
4. World-negating Powers: The sects obsessed with individualist holiness

Alliance with any of the above groups would not render justice to the unorganized ordinary folk (*ptōchoi/ochlos*)[4] who experienced irreparable damage by various dominant groups. Physical torture, guilt feelings, violent blood-shed, and obligatory pollution were the respective painful effects from these powers imposed upon the common people. The common folk that Jesus had alliance with in the public space had no centralized powers, self-righteousness, lethal weapons, or self-pontificating holiness. His active alliance with the broken people empowered them with the dynamic process of gradual politicization awakening them with the spirit of self-confidence and self-empowerment from with.

In contrast to any restricted fellowship with exclusive attitude and colonial dismissal of egalitarianism, the Eucharistic culture set afloat by Jesus had the orientation of voluntary offer of one's life own life for upholding the spirit of *koinonia* for ensuring the union of minds and hearts. Accordingly the love of the neighbour as the uncompromising expression of the love of God demands every human person of good will to become a Good Samaritan to one another. And every person is challenged to become the Son of Man, not to be served but to serve others with the spirit of becoming the ransom for many. This is how the humans could become the human family of co-heirs of one God who is the only Father/ Mother of all brothers and sisters.

The Samaritan women and men, relegated as untouchable creatures are looked upon by the Eucharistic ethos as respectable dialogical partners (Jn 4:1-42). The utmost humanitarian sensitivity of the "untouchable" Samaritan to reach out to the faceless and nameless victim on the roadside is emphasized in contrast to the self-designated "purity" of the priest and the Levite (Lk 10:25-37). Jesus' sensitivity has the courage to publicly acknowledge the Samaritan's spiritual dignity in gratefully acknowledging the gift of healing received from the divine (Lk 17:11-19).

When Jesus' disciples wish to call "fire from heaven" over the Samaritans for not readily welcoming the people of Jewish origins into their villages, they are educated with a rebuke in line with the Eucharistic culture of inclusion (Lk 9:51-55). Similarly, Jesus accepts the great faith of the gentile Canaanite woman and grants her petition (Mt 15:21-28; Mk 7:24-30). In the first Eucharist Jesus willingly offers himself to cleanse the dirty feet of the friends-to-be-sent-as-servants (Jn 13:1-11), emphasising that the "servants are not greater than the master" (Jn 15:20).

The universal salvation for all could be realized only through the salvation of the little flock and the little ones. The culture of power accumulation by Pharaohs, Monarchs, Pilates, and Herods has been dismissed and every powerless empty stomach is to be been filled with abundant gifts of divine providence. The self-emptying cross becomes the spring board for the celebration of the empty tomb. This indeed is the power of the powerlessness.

IV Exploration into Encountering Conflict Situation

When the religious intelligentsia in collaboration with social elite indulged in unbridled commercial activities inside the temples, he drove them out with prophetic courage. In other words, Jesus resisted the commercialization of the divine and the commoditization of the humans. "As a raging egalitarian, an invincible socialist, an economic democrat, Jesus believed that the divine embrace is meant for all nations and peoples"[5] through the humanization of the excluded masses (*ochlos*).

In such conflict-situations the perspectives of the ruling elite and subordinated people run counter to each other. If the powerless organize themselves for claiming their rights, the dominant unleash layers of violence upon them. And here one needs to comprehend the trajectory of Jesus for encountering violence from subaltern soil. The life-affirming praxis of Jesus manifested the following trends of subaltern sensibilities with conflicting orientations.[6] (See table on page 49.)

In the above conflicting orientations, Jesus cannot be eternally fixated with either one or other orientations as shown above while encountering violence. He could be located in both the sectors at ease. But what mattered to him was the uncompromising criterion of promoting and protecting life when it is endangered. And obviously, we find that Jesus was not having

Jesus' Life and Mission

Benign Conventional Approaches	Assertive Counter-cultural Approaches
Forgiving others seven times seventy (Mt 18:21-22)	All sins will be forgiven but not those against the Holy Spirit (Mk 3:28-30)
Forgive them O Lord for they know not what they do (Lk 23:34)	Lashing the traders and money-exchangers out from the temple premises (Jn 2:13-16)
Show your left cheek to be slapped (Mt 5:39)	Why did you slap me? (Jn 18:23)
Keeping silence during Pilate's enquiry (Jn 19:9)	Retorting during Pilate's enquiry (Jn 18:36-37; 19:11)
The kingdom of heaven is like mustard seed and leaven (Mt 13:31-33)	The kingdom of heaven suffers violence (Mt 11:12)
Law is to be fulfilled to the last iota (Mt 5:17-20)	Going beyond the Law- It is said in the Law but now I tell you (Mt 5:21-43)
Supremacy of the Law (Mt 22:34-40)	Law for the promotion of life (Mk 2:23-28; 3:1-6)
The time is not yet come (Jn 2:4)	The time has come (Jn 4:21)
I will not leave you as orphans (Jn 14:18)	For not thinking like God Get! Behind me Satan (Mk 8:33)
Put down your sword into the sheath (Jn 18:11)	Buy a sword and two are enough (Lk 22:36, 38)
One cannot at once serve God and mammon (Lk 16:13)	Gather friends even with unjust riches (Lk 16:9)
Intense personal prayers for day and night (Mk 1:35; 6:46; 14:32-38)	Those who cry 'Lord! Lord!' cannot enter the Kingdom of Heaven (Mt 7:21)
Get reconciled on the way (Mt 5:25-26)	Remove the dust off the leg when rejected (Lk 10:11)
Personal prayer in privacy (Mt 6:6; Lk 6:12)	Wide and effective proclamation of the Reign of God (Mk 1:38-39; Mt 28:19)
Surrounded by crowds of people (Mk 1:45; 3:10; 6:54-56)	Escaping from the crowds of people (Jn 6:15)
Humans do not live by bread alone (Lk 4:4)	Being perceived as glutton and drunkard (Lk 7:34)

the leisure of meticulously evolving the discourses on the virtues of non-violence or the vices of violence as the starting point of getting engaged with life-struggles.

The paschal event of the resurrection of the crucified Jesus Christ is the assertive dismissal of the divine against the growing culture of torture. It manifests a zero tolerance towards the human persecution against other humans. Jesus' definitive choice of the mercy for the sinners against the worship of the self-righteousness (Mt 9:13) is eloquently lived out before and after his death. When the ruling elite are keen in sacrificing someone else for the sake of many (Jn 11: 45-53), Jesus dares to voluntarily offer his very life as the ransom for many (Mk 10:45). This theological perception seems to be spontaneously portrayed in the act of his loud protest against harming his disciples amidst the chaos of his arrest at Gethsemane (Jn 18:8-9).

The process of 'taking away the sins of the world' entails an on-going struggle for anyone who will be thrown into the conflict situation. Every genuine accompaniment with the marginalized people by the field activists or organic intellectuals places them at loggerheads with the ruling elite. While the impoverished women, men, and children are further pauperised through various systemic evils, we need insightful vision and inspiring mission for empowering them to lead a dignified life as co-creators with God, co-workers with other humans and co-born with Nature. This exploration undertaken in dialogue with the power discourse in the life and mission of Jesus could lead us along the path of promoting contemplative action and compassionate justice.

V Conclusion: Empowering the Disempowered

The disempowered people are, often, dismissed as the objects by the ruling elite. But Jesus seemed to have deployed all his inner powers to instil a sense of assertive self-respect from deep within by subverting the socio-cultural hegemony imposed by the dominant classes of his times. He identified the evocative symbol of 'reign of God' to evolve the spirit of religio-cultural assertion of the subaltern people with his alliance for egalitarianism with them. In every conflict-ridden situation defeating the voiceless people with cumulative violence, Jesus opted for the politico-cultural strategy of protecting and promoting their life, even with the risk of giving up his own life. The ethics of egalitarianism, the aesthetics of solidarity and empowerment with humanization seem to constitute the core of the community-building agenda of Jesus seeking to democratize the power to all.

Bibliography

A. Byung-Mu, 'Jesus and the Minjung in the Gospel of Mark', in Rasiah S. Sugirtharajah, *Voices from the Margin: Interpreting the Bible in the Third World*, Maryknoll: Orbis, 2016.

V. R. Krishna Iyer, 'Remembering a Glorious Rebel'. *The Hindu- Daily Newspaper*, Chennai Edition, December 24 (2008).

D. Karr, God with Us. A Bold Understanding of Suffering, *Jesus Christ and Forgiveness*, Chennai: The Christian Literature Society, 2018.

A. M. A. Raja, 'The Authority of Jesus: A Dalit Reading of Mk 11:27-33', *Jeevadhara* 25 (1995), 123-138.

A. M. A. Raja, 'Subaltern Exploration into Encountering Violence', in S. Mulackal and A. R. Lazar (eds.), *Violence in Today's Society: Indian Theological Reflections*, Bangalore: Asian Trading Corporation, 2012, 1-21.

Notes

1. D. Karr, God with Us. *A Bold Understanding of Suffering, Jesus Christ and Forgiveness*, Chennai: The Christian Literature Society, 2018, 69-86.
2. A. M. A. Raja, 'The Authority of Jesus: A Dalit Reading of Mk 11:27- 33', *Jeevadhara* 25 (1995), 123-138.
3. V. R. Krishna Iyer, 'Remembering a Glorious Rebel'. *The Hindu- Daily Newspaper*, Chennai Edition, December 24 (2008).
4. A. Byung-Mu, Jesus and the Minjung in the Gospel of Mark, in Rasiah S. Sugirtharajah, *Voices from the Margin: Interpreting the Bible in the Third World*, Maryknoll: Orbis, 2016, 145-161.
5. V. R. Krishna Iyer, 'Remembering a Glorious Rebel'. *The Hindu- Daily Newspaper*, Chennai Edition, December 24 (2008).
6. A. Maria Arul Raja, 'Subaltern Exploration into Encountering Violence', in Shalini Mulackal and A. Roy Lazar (eds.), *Violence in Today's Society: Indian Theological Reflections*, Bangalore: Asian Trading Corporation, 2012, 1-21.

The Power of the Law – the Law of Power: On the Significance of Canon Law for Issues of Power in the Church

JUDITH HAHN

As in any legal system, power plays an essential role in canon law, in two respects. The power of law indicates the central significance of law in building and shaping society. As the law of power, it puts forward rules that create authority and assign competences within a community governed by law. The authority (power) thus created, however, needs legitimation if it is to be respected in the community. This in turn takes place in the modern era first and foremost through law: power counts as legitimate when it is limited by law. The fact that this rule of law has been undermined in the Church is currently putting canon law under pressure and raising questions about its legitimacy.

If we are going to talk about power and law, three things need to be clarified first. What power means and what law means has to be established, and a connection has to be made between power and law. This is made more difficult by the fact that power is an extremely controversial concept in the social sciences;[1] the sociologist Steven Lukes calls it an 'essentially contested concept'.[2] To talk about power demands a choice for one of the developed concepts of power. For a study of the connection between power and law the analysis of power produced by Niklas Luhmann has the advantage not only that Luhmann used a concept in which power and law related to each other, but also that he established a strong relationship between the two.

I Power, law and their connections

Luhmann, in his definition, maintained 'that power is a chance to increase the probability that improbable sets of circumstances will come to pass'.[3] His formulation echoes Max Weber's famous phrase when he defined power as 'the probability that one actor within a social relationship will be able to carry out his own will despite resistance, regardless of the basis on which this probability rests'.[4] Unlike Weber, however, Luhmann does not dwell on the opposition to the exercise of power from those subject to it, but considers how power makes choices. He argues that to choose from the available possibilities of an action one that is not obvious is evidence of power.[5] Those subordinated to power overwhelmingly tolerate its exercise, although they too seek to exclude alternative possibilities such as sanctions. Luhmann notes: 'Avoiding (possible and possibly permanent) sanctions is essential to the function of power.'[6] He explains how power operates: power 'ensures that various causal chains are available independently of the will of those subject to power and their actions – whether they want this or not.'[7] This independence of the exercise of power from the will of its subordinates has a lesser tendency to violence in Luhmann than, for example, in Weber. He emphasises that 'the causality of power consists in the neutralising of the will of the subjects, not necessarily in breaking it. It affects them if and only if they wanted to act in the same way and then discover that they have to anyway.'[8]

By law Luhmann means a 'structure...based on the coherent generalisation of normative expectations of behaviour'.[9] Whereas many definitions start from the idea that law steers behaviour, Luhmann attributes less weight to behaviour. He says of law: 'Its primary function lies not in producing specific behaviour, but in strengthening specific expectations.'[10] Law is a set of norms in which 'it can be expected that normative expectation is expected as a norm'.[11] Nonetheless this structure of expectation is not sufficient to identify law, because it applies to all norms. Law is distinct from other norms is being the communications that can be identified through the code right/wrong.

Luhmann also uses binary codes to explain the connection between power and law. Power is coded primarily as power/powerlessness, but it also uses a second coding. This takes place 'in our tradition through the binary model of right and wrong'.[12] Elsewhere Luhmann speaks of a 'double nature of power codes, consisting of strength/weakness and right/wrong'.[13] In so doing he shows that in the case of power in modern Western societies, he sees behind the exercise of power by direct action on others a structurally supported second level operating: the exercise of power through law. He comments: 'Everyday life in a society is determined by recourse to normalised power, namely the power of law, to a much greater degree than by the brutal and selfish use of power.'[14] As the 'normal form' in which people encounter power from day to day, the power of law is a force that directs social intercourse.[15]

According to Luhmann, the power of law represents a high degree of 'technical input into power'.[16] This is because law gives power the possibility of 'relatively context-free application'.[17] Luhmann presents law in this sense as a borrowed power gap, in the sense that it creates power relations that would not result from a direct confrontation: 'In situations in which neither of the participants has clear power over the other by virtue of their own sources of power, but draws on a clear power gap based on a ruler outside the situation and mediated by the law. Whoever has the law on their side in the situation also has power to mobilise power.'[18] Luhmann accordingly calls law 'an alarm bell to alert the ruler'.[19]

This connection between power and law can be studied on many levels. This article will offer two perspectives on canon law, *the power of law and the law of power*. Discussion of the *power of law* relates to the social significance of law as a particular type of power phenomenon. Reference to the law of power emphasises that law generates power relations, by effecting an attribution of power. Both dynamics, the power of law and the law of power, are associated with any legal system,[20] canon law included.[21] The power of canon law and its use of power are currently facing criticism. The reasons for this will also have to be discussed in terms of the theory of power.

II The power of canon law

The powerful impact of canon law is part of its societal influence; it is a hugely powerful social phenomenon. Law shapes reality. It is ubiquitous in human social relationships, even if often invisible or concealed. It creates subjects: in many cases law creates the subjects whose activity it regulates.[22] This is explained by legal philosopher Ronald Dworkin in his study *Law's Empire*, in which he describes the expanding dominance of law in modern societies, as it penetrates politics, ethics and other areas:

> We live in and by the law. It makes us what we are: citizens and employees and doctors and spouses and people who own things. It is sword, shield, and menace: we insist on our wage, or refuse to pay our rent, or are forced to forfeit penalties, or are closed up in jail, all in the name of what our abstract and ethereal sovereign, the law, has decreed [...]. We are subjects of law's empire.[23]

Canon law is also powerful in this way. Anyone active in the sphere of the Church finds that they are in legal space. Church structures rest on law. It is on the foundation of law that decisions are made about who is a lay person or a cleric, what conditions are required to become a cleric and how this takes place. What powers office-holders in the Church have depends on law. Who has access to the sacraments and who doesn't is determined by law. Many of these regulations are based on Church doctrine, but it is only by means of law that they are generalised, solidify into structures and become part of the Church's organisational make-up.

The power of the Church's canon law is obvious, but nevertheless not without problems. It is currently clear from numerous cases that canon law has forfeited credibility in all sorts of areas. It is losing force as its influence on social reality and relationships between Church members in the Western churches disappears. Canon law remains effective as an instrument to maintain structures, but its importance in the lives of the faithful is gradually diminishing. Canonical prohibitions or regulations are frequently ignored. For example, very few Catholics in the industrialised countries feel obliged to observe the obligation to go to confession once a year (cf Canon 989/CIC 1983), or, if they do, it is hardly because the *law* requires it. If Church authorities hear of breaches of canon law, as a rule they take no action. Hardly any bishop would take it into his head to begin a canonical procedure against Catholic parents who had their children baptised in a different denomination (cf Canon 1366 CIC 1983). Options offered by canon law are also decreasingly taken up. Whether we are dealing with Church marriage or nullity proceedings, at least in Western countries, demand for canonical institutions or offers of canonical assurance is in decline. Canonical guidelines overwhelmingly exist only on paper. With the exception of abuse cases, canonical sanctions are rarely considered, and the same is true of civil suits. Applications for a declaration of nullity have a role, but in the German-speaking countries this is almost exclusively among Church members in Church employment who fear that a second marriage would have consequences for their employment status.

So the influence of canon law is receding markedly. What it means when law's power diminishes can be examined in Luhmann. He regards two phenomena as responsible for law's loss of power, inflation and deflation of power. Power inflation occurs as a result of 'the devaluation of motivational factors',[24] for example, as a result of 'a style of communication that operates with threats that are either empty or only rarely come to anything'.[25] Threats of Church penalties that in the vast majority of cases come to nothing are a sign of an inflation of canon law. The converse, a deflation of power, goes with 'a failure to make use of opportunities to generalise, with the disadvantage that possibilities for application are not used'.[26] A canon law that gives Church members inadequate guarantees of freedom, has no clear procedure, and fails in dealing with crimes of abuse displays signs of deflation. In the areas affected it is exposed as a powerless regulator for the Church as a community governed by the rule of law.

These problems of canon law have an effect on its acceptance. As the status of the law declines, so does the willingness of Church members to follow it. Their attitude to it is often one of rejection. That too is a way of exercising power. Church members show their power by ignoring inflationary law and object to the deflationary failure to make use of legal opportunities.

III Church law on power

This disapproval has not a little to do with Church law on power, the canonical rules dealing with the distribution of Church power. The reason is that the attribution of power in the Church largely depends on a criterion that is being increasingly questioned, membership of the clerical state. A person who holds power in the Church, is said to enjoy *potestas*. This concept includes two forms of authority, the authority of order and the authority of leadership, which are linked. The power of order conveyed through priestly or episcopal ordination (*potestas ordinis*) – the ability to perform sacramental acts in the liturgy that are reserved to ordained persons – forms the condition for occupying positions that enjoy leadership authority *(potestas jurisdictionis* or *regiminis*), that is, authority for governance in the Church.

Canon 129 § 1 CIC/1983 says: 'Those who have received sacred orders are qualified, according to the norm of the prescripts of the law, for the power of governance.' From this it follows that 'Only clerics can obtain offices for whose exercise the power of orders or the power of ecclesiastical governance is required' (c. 274 § 1 CIC/1983). Lay women and men are described under current law as able to 'cooperate in the exercise of this same power according to the norm of law' (Can. 129 § 2 CIC/1983). What 'cooperate' (*cooperari* in the Latin) means is, however, unclear. The prefix co- identifies the possibilities of action for lay women and men as joining in with what clerics do, but what possibilities are included is left unspoken. Different interpretations of the rule are in circulation. While a good many commentators insist that the cooperation of the laity is limited to preparatory or auxiliary tasks alongside the clerical activity, others interpret *cooperari* as independent and responsible collaboration in achieving the Church's aims.

Although it might seem urgent to clarify the meaning of this concept to understand the authority of lay women and men in the Church, to date the supreme authority in the Church has not yet deigned to define the scope of lay power more closely. Canonist Hubert Socha is almost apologetic in his explanation that the lack of clarity is due to canonical ignorance about the internal structure of the Church. He suggests that canonical ambiguity is necessary 'to deal with the question of the structure of this authority, which has not yet been elucidated theologically'.[27]

This canonical silence can also be judged more critically. The nebulous position of canon law on the question of the competences of lay women and men enables decision-makers in the Church to take advantage of this uncertainty; it gives them and their exercise of power maximum scope. As long as there is doubt about what lay women and men are capable of, any Church authority can decide for himself how to interpret the rule. In a local Church where the leadership of lay women and men is needed, *cooperari* promises autonomy and responsibility. In a local Church with sufficient clergy, preparatory tasks and assistance is all that's on offer. As this example shows, power can easily slide into authoritarianism. Ambiguous law allows arbitrary decision-making.

A further peculiarity of Church law on power is that it only restricts and checks power to a limited degree. Canon law has no separation of powers. The consequence of this is that legislative, judicial and executive power lie in the hands of the same members of the hierarchy. There is a functional division of powers (cf Can. 391 § 1 CIC/1983), but this is justified by exclusively practical reasons (cf Can. 391 § 2 CIC/1983) and does not have the clear separation of powers found in modern civil constitutions. The power vested in the pope, the college of bishops and the diocesan bishop (cf Cann. 331, 336, 381 CIC/1983) is not differentiated democratically but combined in an absolutist way.

Even today the Church uses authority models from the early modern era, as the canonists Nobert Lüdecke and Georg Bier illustrate: 'Church law is understood phenomenologically and structurally as analogous to law in the state, however not to law in the modern democratic constitutional state but to the absolutist authoritarian state of the modern era.'[28] The absolutist legal structure culminates in a monarch at the pinnacle, who is only morally restrained, and brings about the common good,'[29] and so is largely free from effective third-party influence. A diocesan bishop in his diocese enjoys 'all ordinary, proper, and immediate power which is required for the exercise of his pastoral function except for cases which the law or a decree of the Supreme Pontiff reserves to the supreme authority or to another ecclesiastical authority' (Can. 381 § 1 CIC/1983). This reveals immense authority, though it is limited. It is limited functionally to the power necessary to the exercise of the office of a bishop and relationally limited in that episcopal power has a limit in the divisions of competence found in universal Church law that benefit other authorities.

The situation of the Pope is different. He is given 'supreme, full, immediate, and universal ordinary power', which he 'which he is always able to exercise freely'
(Can. 331 CIC/1983). That this indicates a largely unrestricted power is shown in the Church's procedural law, which exempts papal action from judicial review (cf Can. 1404 CIC/1983). Thus in the case of the Pope the question arises whether and how far canon law binds him, if at all.

He is limited in the exercise of his office by divine law. Yet what divine law entails is defined by the Pope himself. Lüdecke und Bier emphasise: 'What is required by the office of pope is decided by the Pope himself in responsibility before God.'[30] They note that this includes the decision as to whether and how the pope's authority is limited. True, the Pope may be morally bound to observe canon law. If he fails to do so, however, he need fear no sanctions. There is no legal authority that could prevent him from setting himself above the law of the Church.

IV Conclusion

As we have seen, Church law on power exercises only a very weak check on power. The fact that Church authorities are hardly faced with the modern civil resources of the separation of powers may at first sight make them seem more powerful than secular leaders, but their power cannot escape a suspicion of illegitimacy. In its openness to the arbitrary exercise of power and absolutist accumulation of power, Church law on power raises questions among Church members. In terms of the sociology of power this is only to be expected, as we can see from Luhmann's work. In our culture there is an assumption that 'a person in power has a rule-based, legal and moral tie to his power'.[31] From the point of view of legitimacy, someone who exercises power in the form of legal power must not, according to Luhmann, act arbitrarily, but must accept 'consistency constraints'.[32] It is a characteristic of power in modern Western societies that 'a normative form of legitimation or even a fully worked out definition of power puts increased pressure on the leader to be consistent'.[33] Power is deprived of its 'elasticity in use' as those who possess it are only rarely 'allowed to act opportunistically'.[34] This explains why law – quite irrespective of its content -, primarily through its own power to curb political power, the so-called 'rule of law', produces legitimacy. Law proves that power is legitimate by limiting and controlling it.

Power, then, in the modern era demonstrates that it deserves respect by accepting the limits of law. In contrast, its legitimacy dwindles to the degree that law does not bind those in power, but leaves scope for absolutist arbitrary rule. An inadequate separation of powers, minimal checks on power, fragmentary restraints on Church authorities on law and statute undermine the rule of law and contribute to weaken the legitimacy of canon law.

It is therefore hardly surprising that Church authorities are noticeably reluctant to connect power and law. They are unwilling to discuss power. Quite often it is hidden behind other concepts, for example dressed up in the terminology of service. Francis, for example, emphasises that it is a primary task of the pope 'to remind everyone that authority in the Church is a service'.[35]

This makes theological sense – and yet it leaves an unpleasant taste in the mouth. Francis' remark can be seen as symptomatic of attempts to theologise power to distract attention from the power of the Church and power in the Church. Anyone who theologises power away makes it more difficult for members of the Church to identify power structures and criticise asymmetries in power. And they encourage a dubious logic. If power is service, whoever has more power performs a greater service.

This prompts two questions. Steven Lukes made the important point that power has to be understood in two senses, as 'power to' and 'power over'. The second especially, Lukes remarks, tends to drop out of sight.[36] This seems to be the case in canon law. We think about 'power to' as authority, competence or empowerment for service to the Church and its members. In the process, however, we are happy to forget or ignore the fact that power is always also 'power over' other people. It provides a foundation for relationships of domination over others. Let us leave on one side the question whether the person who has more power serves more. It is certainly beyond doubt that the person who has more power dominates other people more. That should never be forgotten in any theology of power.

Steven Lukes' theory of power also yields another useful suggestion. Lukes emphasises that power is always linked with responsibility. 'The point [...] of locating power is to fix *responsibility* for consequences held to flow from the action, or inaction, of certain specifiable agents.'[37] With regard to canon law Rainer Bucher translated this idea into the demand that the power of canon law should be exposed, since this would include an identification of the responsible actors: 'We find that raising the question of power means asking, Who is responsible for canon law?'[38] If there is supposed to be some truth in the idea that the person who has more power performs a greater service, this should have the result that the person who has more power should also bear more responsibility for the Church and its faithful. And yet this connection has so far not been sufficiently clear. In Germany at least, no diocesan bishop has yet seen the conspicuous failure of those in power in the Church in dealing with cases of abuse as a reason, as a sign of his great responsibility, to distance himself from power and resign his office.

Translated by Francis McDonagh

Notes

1. See, among others, Niklas Luhmann, *Macht* (Stuttgart, 1975), pp 1–2.
2. See Steven Lukes, Power. *A Radical View*, (Basingstoke 2005), pp 110–124, who cites Walter Bryce Gallie, *Essentially Contested Concepts*, in: *Proceedings of the Aristotelian Society* 56 (1956), 167–198.
3. Luhmann, *Macht*, p. 12.
4. Max Weber, *Wirtschaft und Gesellschaft. Grundriß der verstehenden Soziologie*, ed Johannes Winckelmann. 5th rev. ed. (Tübingen, 1972), p. 27. [English ed: *Economy and Society: An Outline of Interpretive Sociology* (Oakland, 1978)]
5. See Luhmann, *Macht*, pp 22-23.
6. Luhmann, p. 23.
7. Luhmann, p. 11.
8. Luhmann, pp 11-12.
9. Niklas Luhmann, *Rechtssoziologie* (Wiesbaden, 2008), p. 105.
10. Niklas Luhmann, 'Positivität des Rechts als Voraussetzung einer modernen Gesellschaft', in: *Jahrbuch für Rechtssoziologie und Rechtstheorie* 1 (1970), 175–202, 179–180.
11. Niklas Luhmann, *Das Recht der Gesellschaft* (Frankfurt am Main, 1993), p. 144.
12. Luhmann, *Macht*, p. 34.
13. Luhmann, *Macht*, p. 65.
14. Luhmann, *Macht*, p. 17.
15. A considerable number of present-day authors critcise this as the pathology of making social issues legal issues. Among current German-speaking critics, see Christoph Menke, *Kritik der Rechte* (Berlin, 2015); Daniel Loick, *Juridismus. Konturen einer kritischen Theorie des Rechts* (Berlin, 2017).
16. Luhmann, *Macht*, p. 48.
17. Luhmann, *Macht*, p. 48.
18. Luhmann, pp 48-49.
19. Luhmann, p. 49.
20. On the significance of both perspectives for civil law, see e.g. Georg Zenkert,'Die Macht des Rechts – das Recht der Macht', in: Volker Gerhardt et al. (ed.), *Politisches Denken*. Jahrbuch 2011, (Berlin, 2011, 11–24.

21. The connection between canon law and power is, I admit, rarely discussed, and is often overlooked even by canon lawyers. This is a very valid point made to me once by the pastoral theologian Rainer Bucher; see Rainer Bucher, 'Noch ziemlich rücksichtsvoll', in: *Lebendige Seelsorge* 69/3 (2018), 168–169. I regard the present article therefore as an attempt to throw light on this blind spot in canon law.
22. On the connection of power and the creation of subjects, see Michel Foucault, 'Subjekt und Macht', in: Foulcault, *Analytik der Macht*, ed. Daniel Defert and François Ewald, 5th ed., (Frankfurt am Main, 2013), pp 240–263.
23. Ronald Dworkin, *Law's Empire* (Oxford, 1998), p. vii.
24. Luhmann, *Macht*, p. 89.
25. Luhmann, *Macht*, p. 89.
26. Luhmann, *Macht*, p. 89.
27. Hubert Socha, Commentary on Can. 129, in: Klaus Lüdicke (ed), *Münsterischer Kommentar zum Codex Iuris Canonici* (Essen, 2017), 7 Rdnr. 5.
28. Norbert Lüdecke and Georg Bier, *Das römisch-katholische Kirchenrecht. Eine Einführung*, with assistance from Bernhard Sven Anuth (Stuttgart, 2013), p. 26.
29. Norbert Lüdecke and Georg Bier, *Das römisch-katholische Kirchenrecht. Eine Einführung*, (Stuttgart, 2013), p. 26.
30. Norbert Lüdecke and Georg Bier, *Das römisch-katholische Kirchenrecht. Eine Einführung*, p. 118.
31. Luhmann, *Macht*, p. 47.
32. Luhmann, *Macht*, p. 47.
33. Luhmann, p. 28.
34. Luhmann, p.28.
35. *Address of his Holiness Pope Francis for the Conclusion of the Third Extraordinary General Assembly of the Synod of Bishops*, 18 October 2014: http://w2.vatican.va/content/francesco/en/speeches/2014/october/documents/papa-francesco_20141018_conclusione-sinodo-dei-vescovi.html
36. Lukes, Power. *A Radical View*, esp. p. 163.
37. Lukes, Power, p. 58.
38. Rainer Bucher, 'Noch ziemlich rücksichtsvoll', in: *Lebendige Seelsorge* 69/3 (2018), 169.

From the New Political Theology to Critical Political Ethics

HILLE HAKER

Building upon the tradition of the New Political Theology and liberation, decolonial, and feminist theology, this article explores the consequences of a decolonial epistemology of theology for ethical theory. It introduces a critical political ethics that concurs with critical, post-structural, and decolonial theory that knowledge and ethics is necessarily situated while standing firm in their ethical orientation towards liberation from injustice. In all these approaches, the question of freedom is of central importance for the development of political ethics, and political theology as well as critical theory raise the question of authority. Rather than presupposing the liberal concept of autonomy or Kant's moral freedom, critical political ethics distinguishes between four dimensions of freedom, namely transcendental, existential, social, and political freedom. For ethics, the realignment of political theory and practice means that solidarity with the suffering individual and/or group is not only the criterion of moral judgment but also a priority of action. Additionally, however, critical political ethics situates theological ethics in the tradition of witnesses of faith that serve as reference for a creative reimagination of moral and political practices.

I Political Theology as Critique and Struggle for Liberation from Injustice[1]

In its foundational reflection, theological ethics must certainly position itself in relation to the two dominant modern concepts of freedom, namely the Anglo-American concept of liberty and the Kantian concept of moral autonomy. Theology emphasizes that the self is derivative (*abkünftig*) and inscrutable (*unergründlich*), rendering the human being vulnerable as well as open to others. Freedom must attend to the derivatedness (*Abkünftigkeit*) and inscrutability (*Unergründlichkeit*) of human subjectivity and the vulnerability and openness of the human being. Religions position humans in relation to an otherness that, paradoxically, cannot be named and still is given a name – one that will be infinitely questioned. Christianity, like Judaism and Islam, positions the humans in a relation to God, in an address that constitutes meaning but also calls for a response. Following Metz' programmatic New Political Theology rather than Carl Schmitt's political theology in the 1970s and 1980s, theologians have given freedom a critical twist, relating it to the liberation from oppression. In this, the New Political Theology coincided with liberation theology, feminist, black, postcolonial, and decolonial theologies. In their interpretation of the "authority of God," these approaches insist that authority itself is paradoxical, derived from the vulnerable individual, groups, or peoples, and not resting on the sovereignty of political-theological leadership, as the Schmittian tradition argued. Critical theory pointed theology and ethics to a normativity that departs as much from a metaphysical ontotheological order of being as from the naturalism of modern sciences that pretend to be value-free. Horkheimer had claimed as early as 1937 that critical theory, in contrast to traditional (empirical and positivist) theory reflects the situatedness of any knowledge that constitutes at the same time an "interest" or direction of practical philosophy, namely the struggle against oppression, alienation, and the domination of nature, including human nature, through instrumental and technical reason.[2] Critical theory opposes those concepts of rationality that ignore the paradoxical status of the human as derivative, inscrutable, vulnerable, and agential. The group that formed the Frankfurt School in the 1930s was proven right in their critique of instrumental reason and authoritarianism: Western modern thinking had not prevented the Great War of 1914-1918. It did not prevent the rise of several fascist dictatorships in Europe, and it did not prevent the rise of Hitler in Germany. Instrumental rationality was exploited for the *industrial* killing of Jews and any declared "other" in the Nazi deathcamps, and the detonation of two nuclear bombs on the cities of Hiroshima and Nagasaki by the US military. The verdict of critical theory was dire: the history of the 20th century demonstrated the "eclipse of reason" rather than its progress.[3] The "dialectic of enlightenment" pointed to an immanent and unresolved problem of modern thinking.[4]

Similar to critical theory, the New Political Theology aimed at changing the underlying epistemology of its own field, theology, in order to make room for a transformation of theological practices. It centred on the suffering human person, and its own historical roots called for a break with Christian anti-Judaism as well as antisemitism. My own approach takes up both schools, critical theory and political theology, however attending more closely to the consequences for theological ethics. For critical political ethics, the realignment of theory and practice means that solidarity with the suffering individual and/or group is not only the criterion of moral judgment but also the *priority* that must guide Christian personal and political action. It may well be difficult at times to distinguish between suffering that stems from bad luck and suffering from injustice, as Judith Shklar has argued,[5] but it is exactly for this reason that political theology must be complemented by a political *ethics* that addresses the questions of ethical judgments more thoroughly than this has been the case so far.

II Critical Political Ethics

Critical political ethics is opposed to any political-ethical decisionism because it fosters political authoritarianism. It takes up the postmodern critique of a foundational ethics when or insofar as this is immune to critique. It joins the critical deconstruction of truth claims and genealogies of ethical concepts that have contributed to the colonialist epistemology of superiority and inferiority among human beings, groups, and peoples.[6] Yet, as necessary as these analyses are, they are not sufficient from a political-ethical perspective, because it is not clear how they can motivate political-ethical actions: *Not* to play along in the cruel game of planetary destruction may well be an act of resistance, but actions are in part based on the ends that agents set. In the political realms, agents act together, aiming at collective ends that require particular means, strategies, cooperation, and coordination. If critical theory is correct, there is a certain drive to conformity and normalization that must be actively resisted: not to look the other way but to stand up requires political scrutiny, political-ethical virtues, allies who will take the role of political kin, and perseverance. It takes courage to stand up for one's rights, for the rights of others, and for anybody to have the right to have rights. The role of *ethics* with respect to political practices is not to be confused with the moral practices, however. Rather, ethics must preserve its critical role of reflecting practices and subjecting them to the analysis of their normative justifications, as Ricœur aptly states in a comment to Habermas' discourse ethics:

> One might say, with Habermas, that the philosopher should not hold a discourse of citizens—practical discourse—but a discourse on the discourse of citizens—a discourse no longer practical, but critical—and that this critical discourse calls for reference to a regulatory idea which itself lays claim to truth and no longer to opinion.[7]

Following this argument, critical political ethics cannot evade the question of normativity and moral truth. If, however, theological ethics cannot return to an epistemology that points to divine law as legitimization of a particular kind of politics, morally justified by the sovereign authority of the Magisterium, what other route can ethics take?[8] I believe that a *reflective* justification of normative claims is possible, as long as this justification is either strictly formal or remaining open to infinite questioning when turning to substantial claims.[9] Kant's ethics is indispensable in the universalization of moral claims regarding the dignity and freedom of human beings, which constitutes equality and reciprocity between agents. Yet, the concept of freedom does not only concern autonomy. I want to distinguish between four dimensions of freedom that need to be kept in play. I call them transcendental, existential, social, and political, and I claim that none of them must be discarded in ethical reasoning: *First*, Kant rightly showed that freedom is the foundational, *transcendental* concept of morality, i.e. agents' capability to be held responsible for one's actions. It does not exclude obligations towards those who are not agents, or the environment, for instance. Rather, it establishes the concept of responsibility as implication of moral agency. Autonomy in this sense is not merely the liberty to choose the courses of action but also the susceptibility to blame and praise by others who may hold the agents accountable and demand certain actions from them. *Second*, the existentialist interpretation of freedom from Kierkegaard to Sartre, de Beauvoir, and Camus entails the self-determination captured in the liberal autonomy concept but also goes beyond it. It stresses freedom as an *existential* concept that is captured in the concept of ethical identity. Freedom in this understanding is an infinite existential task of becoming oneself, of acknowledging the dynamic, future-oriented project of one's biography that rests, at least in part, upon self-reflective choices one makes for one's life.[10] *Third*, agents are necessarily embedded and entangled in the dialectic of self-other relations. Thus, although it is necessarily personal, freedom is re-active and responsive, constituting relations interconnection, of power, or domination and subjection. Whereas the existentialist tradition in the Hegelian tradition — Sartre especially — emphasizes the power *over* the self that emerges from the self-other relation, others who follow the theory of recognition, explore the spaces of social freedom that enable individuals to interact with each other.[11] Critical political ethics, however, insists that the *denial* of spaces of social freedom, or the exclusion from them, deprive individuals being recognized as subjects and moral agents, and hence are vulnerable to dehumanization by other agents. Because this is more often the reality than not, freedom is therefore, *fourth*, a claim on others, a moral demand to be seen, to be responded to, and to be respected in one's dignity.[12] This demand is reflected in the struggles for liberation from violations of human dignity and structures of violence, which connects it both to the theology of liberation and to the theory of recognition, insofar as the latter addresses the multiple struggles for equal respect.

In theological thinking, the liberation from oppression has been interpreted as a path towards salvation, but reflecting the early modern history of Christianity, critical political ethics acknowledges that missionaries also used the theology salvation, blended with anti-judaist supersessionism and political colonialization, for their own missionary purposes. As a result, colonization is a political as well as a theological concept. Western *Christian* theology provided the narrative that entails, among others, the "racial contract," as Charles Mills has called it,[13] and it is exactly this narrative that is promoted by the Christian Right in the USA today.[14] Critical political ethics must therefore break with a teleological and/or providential theology of salvation that returns as secularized philosophy of progress in history. Likewise, it must break with an apocalyptic theology of the end time and insist on the transformative policies in history. It must break with any political *or* ecclesial view that contradicts the above-mentioned understanding of freedom that embraces the capability to act and be held accountable, the quest for meaning in one's life, the need to act together as persons and collective, and the political struggle for justice and equality.

Unfortunately, the Catholic Church often confuses the legitimacy of the Magisterium's *political-ecclesial* authority of the Church with its assumed sacred authority that renders the Church immune to criticism. Furthermore, it conflates its ecclesial authority with the power to *define* what is morally right or wrong. The Church certainly has its own normative framework: the ecclesial law (Canon Law), comes with a sanctioning power analogous to secular laws, which is legitimate and legitimized by the ecclesial procedures—though often contradictory, insufficient, denigrative of women, but also little known by the faithful. The Catechism is a theologial and moral guide that summarizes and orients the beliefs of the ecclesia—but it is clearly open to criticism, interpretation, and change. Moral normativity, however, functions differently than the Canon Law or the Catechism: encountering a moral demand or claim *coincides* with the experience of moral agency, namely as the inability *not* to perceive the claim that others make on us. Morality entails the experience of the power to act, to take responsibility for one's actions, and/or to be held accountable for them. Reacting to the concept of modern autonomy that it regards as a *threat* to morality, the Church reduces it to the almost unlimited freedom of choice that is, moreover, fostered in secularized liberal democracies. In contrast to this distorted view of freedom, moral agents experience all four dimensions of freedom mentioned above. Kant's concept of autonomy is to a certain degree even compatible with the scholastic tradition of Thomas Aquinas whom the Church emphasizes as one of its most important guides regarding moral reasoning and virtues. The moral demand on Catholics to freely and obediently receive the moral imperatives from the Pope who speaks in the name of God, contradicts the very natural law of reason that Catholic ethics claims to adhere to.

As the moral-theological tradition teaches, moral judgments are situated in concrete histories and traditions. Understanding, too, is necessarily historical, contextual, and experiential. The names and images of God found in the tradition must be examined, potentially critiqued, potentially contested, and reinterpreted, as Derrida argues in his works that I take to establish a critical hermeneutics.[15] Ultimately, no name or image can capture God, nor should that even be the goal of theology. Instead, language is the human way of interpreting one's unique and existential freedom-in-relation, creating a web of belonging to forbearers in faith, one's chosen kin. These include the witnesses of the Son of Man whom God chose as his Son, and whom God chose to become akin to every human. Critical political ethics reminds theological ethics (if not all ethics) that empire imageries — of the sovereign leader within a nation, or the empire nation among all nations — stand opposed to the images of those who have been morally injured by practices and structures of exclusion, racism, poverty, oppression, and isolation. Attesting to God's special bonds with humans in history, Christian theology is reminded of the ongoing history of violence, domination, and exploitation of land and peoples: children, women, and men who are forced to succumb to those who enforce their violence as a political, if not theological right, without ever being blamed or held accountable. Learning from this history, critical political ethics is not only reflective and critical in view of moral practices. It is also *constructive* and *creative*. It seeks in the practices models of freedom that allow agents to break free from oppression, or conformity and complicity with institutional arrangement that constitute exploitation and oppression. In other words: it seeks models that show how engagement for liberation, solidarity, and justice is possible and effective.[16] Critical political ethics contributes to change by listening to the experiences and by imagining new, effective practices, new structures of social action, and potentially new institutional governance structures that are liberating rather than cementing the existing asymmetries between individuals, groups, and nations, together with the people who are most affected by the current structural sins, against humans, animals, and the earth.

Critical political ethics, it seems to me, is needed more than ever today. As theological ethics, it provides sources for political-ethical reasoning that point beyond the reified world. Claiming that the political is always and necessarily personal (though not necessarily private), critical political ethics takes the vulnerable agent as its *starting point*, and the (morally) injured at the *normative centre* of its ethics. Critical political ethics is not naïve, and looking at the history of Christianity, it acknowledges that justice requires struggles. These struggles require the learning of courage, perseverance, and motivation in the midst of futility, as Camus' ethics demonstrates so clearly. It requires the deliberate formation and internalization of political virtues, such as compassion (*Anteilnahme*) and solidarity, and the sensitization for injustice. As Christian ethics, critical political ethics has the experience and the means to foster these political virtues that enable individuals and groups to engage in concrete actions and practices. It seeks to contribute to the development a new habitus of response-ability, formed through the experiences of social, political actions, critically reflected upon in ethical scholarship. Like the theologians of the last third of the 20th century, i.e. political, liberation, feminist and mujerista and womanist, black, postcolonial, and decolonial theologies, took theology to the streets, critical political ethics is connected to the social movements, which it accompanies in critical solidarity. It is an ethics of and for the weekdays: the days of responses to moral injuries, suffering, and often death. Theologians and clergy often linger happily in the vicinity of political power. It must go out into the rubble of the streets, linger among the people whose dreams are being shattered again and again.

Like its kin, the theologians and clergy who have for decades acted in the midst of those on the dark side of the current world disorder, Western theologians and ethicists must not only act; they must themselves unlearn the language and habitus of coloniality, seeking their own response to the alienated, vision-less, individualized people who are also deprived of their own happiness by the global disorder. Like addicts to consumption, they stumble from promise to promise, and from crisis to crisis, often with no expectation that life can have a deeper meaning than consumption and conformity. Theologians and clergy in the West must attend to them to foster personal, social, and political transformation. Critical political ethics cannot discern one response but rather, it will generate *multiple* responses to the moral crises of our time. Furthermore, ethics cannot offer the answer to "the" meaning of human existence, because this is the task of freedom that every human being is endowed with. But Christian ethics can continue to tell the story of past human experiences and past interpretations of God which point to a future that is yet to come. These stories do not mirror the passive, obedient recipients of God's word but the active witnesses of faith. Many witnesses of faith refused to choose between the love of God and the love of humans. Even the central symbol of female submission and obedience in Western Catholicism, Mary, invoked Hannah's song right after the Annunciation, remembering her trust in God who will throw the powerful from their throne, and for this she is loved by millions of Catholics who pray in her name (1 Sam 2:1-10; Luke 1:46-56).

In light of this biblical and theological tradition, the critique of domination and theo-political authoritarianism must include the Catholic Church. Like any institution, it is not exempt from human fallibility and the sin of self-love, love of power and domination. My approach is therefore critical in two ways: it is critical of any *political theory* that legitimizes power over others by invoking the name of God, and of any *theology* that justifies violence and injustice in the name of the sacred power of the Church or, in fact, any religion. Instead, critical political ethics is bound to remember the God who regards the pain of others as her own pain, creating a bond of care that enables humans to trust rather than fear God. This bond breaks the chains, liberating humans to explore their finite, fragile, yet creative freedom together with others. Indeed, this bond does not force moral agents to dismiss their agency, nor violates it their freedom rights. Quite to the contrary, it is a bond that *empowers* humans to struggle with and for others, for liberation and justice.

Bibliography

T. Adorno/M. Horkheimer, *Dialectic of enlightenment*, London: Verso Books, Max. 2016 (orig. 1944).

S. de Beauvoir, *The ethics of ambiguity*, New York: Citadel Press, 1962.

J. M. Bernstein, *Torture and dignity: an essay on moral injury*, Chicago, London: The University of Chicago Press, 2015.

R. Bernstein, "Serious Play: The Ethical-Political Horizon of Jacques Derrida," *The Journal of Speculative Philosophy* 1.2 (1987), 93-117.

J. Derrida, "Uninterrupted Diaglogue: Between two infinities, the poem," *Research in Phenomenology* 34.3-19 (2004).

A. Gewirth, *Reason and morality*, Chicago, London: University of

Chicago Press, 1978.

H. Haker, *The Renewal of Catholic Social Ethics: Towards a Critical Political Ethics*, Würzburg: Echter Verlag, 2020.

C. Hedge, *American Fascists: The Christian Right and the War on America*, New York: Simon & Schuster, 2008.

A. Honneth, *Freedom's Right: The Social Foundations of Democratic Life*, New York: Columbia University Press, 2014.

M. Horkheimer, *Critical theory: Selected essays*, New York: Herder and Herder, 1972.

M. Horkheimer, *Eclipse of reason*, New York: Seabury Press, 1974.

C. W. Mills, *The racial contract*, Ithaca, NY: Cornell University Press, 1997.

P. Ricoeur, *The course of recognition*, Cambridge, MA: Harvard University Press, 2006.

P. Ricœur, *The just*, Chicago: University of Chicago Press, 2000.

J. N. Shklar, *The faces of injustice*, New Haven: Yale University Press, 1990.

I. M. Young, *Responsibility for Justice*, Oxford: Oxford University Press, 2013.

From the New Political Theology to Critical Political Ethics

Notes

1. The following essay relies upon a more thorough development of my approach, spelled out in Hille Haker, *The Renewal of Catholic Social Ethics: Towards a Critical Political Ethics*, Würzburg: Echter Verlag, 2020 especially Chapter 10.
2. M. Horkheimer, *Critical theory: Selected essays*, New York: Herder and Herder, 1972.
3. M. Horkheimer, *Eclipse of reason*, New York: Seabury Press, 1974.
4. T. Adorno/M. Horkheimer, *Dialectic of enlightenment*, London: Verso Books, Max. 2016 (orig. 1944)
5. J. N. Shklar, *The faces of injustice*, New Haven: Yale University Press, 1990.
6. Jacques Derrida has offered multiple works that concretize deconstruction, e.g. of forgiveness, of justice, or universalism more general; Foucault has offered major works on truth regimes, e.g. concerning sexuality, madness, punishment, of policing. Both "paths" are indispensable for any ethical or political analysis and must therefore be taken up by a Christian ethics. They certainly offer a methodology that is akin to Adorno's "negative critique" that the 'new political theology' embraced. J. Derrida, "Uninterrupted Diaglogue: Between two infinities, the poem," *Research in Phenomenology* 34.3-19 (2004).
7. P. Ricœur, *The just*, Chicago: University of Chicago Press, 2000, 29.
8. I have argued this at length in H. Haker, 2020.
9. In his foundational ethics, Alan Gewirth has argued that it is possible to combine the formality of Kant's ethics with substantial claims. While I applaud this approach, it still raises many questions about the meaning of freedom and well-being. Cf. A. Gewirth, *Reason and morality*, Chicago, London: University of Chicago Press, 1978.
10. Cf. for instance, S. de Beauvoir, *The ethics of ambiguity*, New York: Citadel Press, 1962.
10. Cf. A. Honneth, *Freedom's Right: The Social Foundations of Democratic Life*, New York: Columbia University Press, 2014; P. Ricoeur, *The course of recognition*, Cambridge, MA: Harvard University Press, 2006.
11. Cf. J. M. Bernstein, *Torture and dignity: an essay on moral injury*, Chicago, London: The University of Chicago Press, 2015. Cf. Also my interpretation of the concept of vulnerable agency in H. Haker, 2020, Chapter 5.
12. C. W. Mills, *The racial contract*, Ithaca, NY: Cornell University Press, 1997.
13. Cf. for an actual account of American Christian Groups that promote white, Christian supremacy: C. Hedge, *American Fascists: The Christian Right and the War on America*, New York: Simon & Schuster, 2008.
14. Cf. for a critical analysis R. Bernstein, "Serious Play: The Ethical-Political Horizon of Jacques Derrida", *The Journal of Speculative Philosophy* 1.2 (1987), 93-117. For Derrida's hermeneutics cf. J. Derrida, "Uninterrupted Diaglogue: Between two infinities, the poem", *Research in Phenomenology* 34 (2004), 3-19.
15. Iris Marion Young has pointed to the collective, social responsibility for justice, especially when no individual can be blamed for acting immorality, yet as a collective, multiple individuals contribute to institutional injustice. Cf. I. M. Young, *Responsibility for Justice*, Oxford: Oxford University Press, 2013.

Discursive, Socio-Economically Sensitive and Performative: Varieties of Publicly Political Christianity[1]

ANSGAR KREUTZER

The new political theology was not the only product of the 1960s. It was at the same time that the liturgical phenomenon of Political Night Prayer also emerged; this is associated with the name of the famous Protestant theologian, Dorothee Sölle (1929-2003). This article focuses on the link this phenomenon creates between a discursive engagement with political issues on the one hand and Christian symbolic practices within a liturgical framework on the other. Drawing on concepts of the public sphere in the social sciences, it draws attention to the significance of not only discursive but also performative elements (such as rituals, dramas and symbols) for political public space, with which a form of Christianity that regards itself as a political public religion can also connect.

I Introduction: Political Night Prayers 1968

1968: the world is dominated by the Cold War. The USA is dropping devastating napalm bombs on Vietnam. Soviet tanks roll into Czechoslovakia and violently destroy the first growths of the Prague Spring. In West Germany there are demonstrations focused on the events of world politics by students and by young people from other social groups, the so-called 68 generation.[2] Events in international and national politics also resonated in the Christian churches. In Cologne's Antoniterkirche Protestant and Catholic Christians met regularly to 'bring politics into prayer', and 'political night prayers' attracted many people.[3]

Varieties of Publicly Political Christianity

The characteristic feature of political night prayers was the combination of bible readings, meditation, political information and debate in a format essentially defined by liturgy. One of the central figures of the movement, the prominent Protestant theologian Dorothee Sölle (1929-2003), reflected on the activity in her book *Political Theology*.[4] Sölle's crucial argument for a political theology is based on the Enlightenment principle of rationality. In a criticism of her teacher, Rudolf Bultmann, Sölle asks how far the Enlightenment critical rationalism, defended by Bultmann in opposition to his own Christian traditions, should go. Her answer to the question was that theological thinking itself, even of the critical variety inspired by the Enlightenment, must also give a critical account of the social and political conditions under which such theological reflection takes place: 'If we look for the common feature that connects historical-critical theology and political awareness, both share a positive relationship to the Enlightenment, to what Kant called "man's emergence from his self-imposed immaturity". If we start from the premise that enlightenment as the process of this emergence is indivisible, that specific human critical capacities cannot define in advance the objects to which they are applied, then enlightened political awareness comes from the same critical, rational spirit as theological enlightenment.'[5]

It is to the credit of the champions of political night prayer that they did not exclude themselves from the scrutiny of this critical attitude that stretches from the Enlightenment via Bultmann's demythologising theology to the critical questioning of social conditions in which religion and theology have always been involved. In a noteworthy passage from one political night prayers, on the subject of faith and politics, under the heading 'Doubt' we find: 'And yet I ask myself, Is all this right? Does the Church really exist to think about political structures? Isn't the purpose of the Church something quite different, to provide quiet, to create space, in which we experience meditation, celebration, worship? Once we bring politics into the Church, we'll have worries and problems too. Do they want to rob us of this last island of peace? Maybe this is what will bring peace to the world!'[6]

This is where the strengths and limitations of this type of liturgically articulated and experienced political theology become clear. Its central feature is the combination not just of public politics with religious language, but in the blending of the symbolic language of faith, with its emotional load, aesthetically structured and expressive liturgy, with political challenges, debates and consequences. It is the 'proportions of the mixture' of Christian religion and public politics that seeks to give a public meaning to religious symbolic practice that will be the focus of this article. (1) First there will be an outline of an understanding of the public sphere that is prominent in theology, the discursive-deliberative model, associated especially with the name of Jürgen Habermas, but (2) it will be critically expanded to include the two dimensions that tend to be neglected, the *socio-economic* and the *performative*. It is these particular dimensions of the public sphere, however, according to the dominant inspiration, that can provide the basis for a contemporary theology of politics in the public sphere. (3) This will be illustrated by the model of a Church involved publicly in politics, as currently embodied, literally, by Pope Francis. (4) Finally there will be a quick look (outwards) at (once more current political) night prayers, which demonstrate the continuing relevance of Christianity to politics and the public sphere in our time, in our societies and in our churches.

II The discursive-deliberative model of the political public sphere and some critical expansions

2.1 The discursive-deliberative model (Jürgen Habermas)

In both the theory of the public sphere and the use of this in theology, particular attention is given to a specific concept, the model of a discursive-deliberative public sphere put forward by the well-known social philosopher Jürgen Habermas.[7] Its elements include exchange of arguments (discourse) and decisions through discussion (deliberation).[8] In his valuable overview of public theology, Florian Höhne stresses: 'I find particularly profitable for the discussion in the German context the idea of the public sphere...[formulated on the basis of Habermas]...: here public spheres mean (civil society) networks "for the communication of contents and opinions" (Habermas).'[9]

The (justified) influence of the discursive/deliberative model in areas including theology is a result of its very close connection with the foundations and functioning of the democratic state governed by law. For Habermas, the public sphere, especially in its discursive-deliberative version, is a structural necessity for the functioning of parliamentary democracy. As is well known, its core is the division of powers between a parliamentary legislature, an executive composed of government and administration and the regulatory organs of the judiciary: 'The core area of the political system is made up of the familiar institutional complexes of the administration (including the government), the courts and democratic opinion formation and decision-making (with parliamentary bodies, political elections, competition between the parties, etc.).'[10] But surrounding this heart of constitutional democracy there must be – and it is indispensable to its functioning – a public sphere, which may be politically aligned, but is located outside the institutional centre of parliamentary democracy: 'feeder groups, associations and organisations… that, vis à vis parliaments and administrations, and also by recourse to the courts, raise societal problems, make political demands, articulate interests or needs and exert influence on the drafting of legislative proposals or policies'.[11] The central function of this political public sphere is to produce sensitivity to societal emergencies that risk going unnoticed in the institutional political machine through its blindness to its own defects. 'The public sphere is an alarm system with sensors that are non-specific, but sensitive society-wide.'[12] Such a political public sphere, which helps with the functioning, the critique and monitoring of institutional parliamentarism, is translated into infrastructural terms by activists from civil society. They essentially form a web of organisations, unions and associations that belong neither to the sphere of the economy nor to the sphere of state bodies. 'Rather, their institutional core is formed by on a voluntary basis by those non-state and non-economic combinations and associations that anchor the communications structures of the public sphere in the societal component of the life-world."[13] This area of a political public sphere, necessarily taking up a position close to the institutional centre of parliamentary democracy, which becomes a reality in networks of civil society actors, also has, in the Habermas model, a (public) place for churches and religious communities.: 'The spectrum [of civil society groups] extends from associations that represent clearly defined group interests through organisations…and cultural institutions…to "public interest groups"…and churches or charitable organisations.'[14] The prominence of Habermas's discursive-deliberative model in public theology is thus not so surprising.

On the one hand it is located close to the mechanisms of a functioning constitutional democracy, while it gives religious communities a place in the structure of civil society actors in which those who practise a religion can participate publicly in the democratic process with contributions to political discourse and deliberation. Nevertheless there is also a current of criticism against Habermas's model, with suggestions of a need for complementary elements of great relevance for a public political theology.

2.2 The socio-economic conditions for deliberative exchange (Nancy Fraser)

The feminist social philosopher agrees completely with Habermas's idea that there is a discursive-deliberative public sphere that is indispensable to democracy. Nevertheless she raises considerable doubts as to whether Habermas's idea simply functions without problems in the reality of democracies as they exist in practice. Not least as a result of the experiences of the women's movement, Fraser's central concern is that the participation of all in the discursive-deliberative public sphere cannot simply be assumed in advance, but that necessary conditions must be stipulated. With historical and empirical data, Fraser points to the often subtle exclusion from discursive and deliberative public spheres that women, for example, but also lower-status social groups (what she calls 'plebeian groups') have had to endure: 'Women of all classes and ethnicities were removed from official political participation because of the gender status attributed to them, and plebeian men were formally excluded from it because of their property status.'[15] On the basis of these historical experiences Fraser makes the general demand for the creation of socio-economic conditions that make possible *de facto* the political participation of people of different social backgrounds. This also means bringing about of a minimum of socio-economic equality. 'It is more a necessary condition for participatory equality that systematic societal inequalities should be abolished. That does not mean that everyone must have the same income, but it does require an approximate equality incompatible with the relationships of domination and subordination produced by the system.'[16]

2.3 The performative dimension of the public sphere (Jeffrey C. Alexander)

Similarly to Fraser, the US sociologist of culture Jeffrey C. Alexander praises the model of a discursive-deliberative public sphere, but also calls for it to be critically expanded.[17] Alexander also believes that civil society, with its abilities to shape political opinion and decision-making, is central to a functioning democracy. Where Fraser widens the deliberative element of the focus to the socio-economic conditions that make possible participation in discourses and decisions, Alexander stresses the performative, expressive, theatrical aspects of the public sphere, and not merely the discursive. Directly contradicting Habermas, he says, 'Publicness should be seen more in dramaturgical terms.'[18] The function of the public sphere and civil society is similar for both Habermas and Alexander. The public sphere is an 'alarm system', alert to social pathologies, cases of discrimination, social failures, which the web of agencies in the democratic constitutional state, legislature, executive and judiciary, does not catch, perhaps does not even notice. But Alexander thinks the way the alarm system works is different. The public sphere, even in politics, is definitely not merely discursive, a matter of debates, verbal communications, communicative exchange, but (also) one of performances, rituals, dramas: 'This [the formation of public opinion] can happen through the making public of discrimination and exclusion, through public protest against injustice, through 'counter-public' ritualising, staging and dramatisation 'on the public stage' of social conflicts silenced by repression or directly repressed, through symbolic actions as well as through the translation of the relevant issues into public discourse.'[19]

III A performative-inclusive model for a publicly political theology and Church

The current Pope clearly adopts the role of a political figure in the public sphere – in terms of Christian faith.[20] In contrast to any sort of liberal idea that religion is a purely private matter, Francis calls for the participation of religious communities in the public sphere: 'Consequently, no one can demand that religion should be relegated to the inner sanctum of personal life, without influence on societal and national life, without concern for the soundness of civil institutions....'[21] Completely in line with the discursive model of the public sphere, Francis defines the locus of such faith-based socio-political involvement as civil society. So, 'via the Pontifical Council for Justice and Peace, he invites social movements from across the world, and does not merely speak a few words of greeting, but gives a lengthy programmatic address and listens to their concerns'.[22] The specific character of Francis' political theology for the public sphere precisely matches the socio-economic and performative dimensions stressed by Fraser and Alexander.

3.1 Socio-economic dimension: option for the poor
The socio-economic conditions emphasised by Fraser as required for public deliberation, participation and ultimately for a functioning democracy have a deep connection with Francis' reshaping of the option for the poor spelt out in detail by liberation theology.[23] For example, he places the option for the poor that starts out as 'material' into the decisive context of social inclusions and political participation. In his programmatic Apostolic Exhortation *Evangelii Gaudium* he paraphrases the option for the poor and gives it an inclusive tweak: 'There is one sign which we should never lack: the option for those who are least, those whom society discards' (EG 195). Fundamental theologian Jürgen Werbick maintains that Francis' central social model of exclusion and inclusion or involvement is *the* hermeneutical key to understanding the deep structure of his pastoral and theological programme: Francis comes back time and again to this central idea, which is like a constant theme in what he says about God: God is and wants *inclusion*. God achieves it in and through human beings: with them he wants to bring about the inclusion of the excluded and marginalised, so that all may share in the fullness of life.'[24] In his interpretation of the option for the poor in the perspective of social inclusion Francis establishes – just as Frazer does – a connection between material resources and democratic participation. In the invitation to civil society representatives mentioned above, his regular meetings with social movements, Francis addresses the poor, the materially marginalised, as protagonists, and not just objects, of politics: 'You have brought a reality that is often silenced into the presence of God, the Church and all peoples. The poor not only suffer injustice, they also struggle against it! We want

your voices to be heard... Without your presence, without truly going to the edges of society, the good proposals and projects we often hear about at international conferences remain stuck in the realm of ideas and wishful thinking.'[25] In Francis' way of thinking the socio-economic option for the poor, social inclusion and the political participation of the marginalised as protagonists in politics go together. 'The integration of the excluded in the construction of a common future generates a moral thrust that provides the impetus to develop appropriate (i.e., not only formal democratic) structures at local, national and international level.[26]

3.2 The performative dimension: symbolic communication
Francis' interpretation of the option for the poor in terms of inclusivity and democratic participation exemplifies Fraser's connection between socio-economic conditions and opportunities, and Alexander's stress on the performative level of the political public sphere is also central to making a reality of the specific form of public political theology and Church Pope Francis stands for. There can be no doubt that expressive symbolic communication is one of the striking features of this pontificate. Francis' vision of far-reaching economic, social and political inclusion is expressed in symbols that have received much attention. There is the modest life style that indicates closeness to the poor, his visit to the refugees on Lampedusa at the very beginning of his pontificate, the liturgical washing of the feet of prisoners, the symbol *par excellence* of exclusion, every Maundy Thursday.[27]

One sign that Francis' performative style of communicating his messages does indeed resonate with the public is the positive reception given to director Wim Wenders' 2018 film *Pope Francis: A Man of His Word*.[28] Wenders was not interested in making a film about the man Jorge Mario Bergoglio/Pope Francis. What he wanted to do was to put Francis' core message on the screen.[29] His way of translating that visually was to have the Pope speaking direct to camera, that is, 'looking straight at the audience', delivering his message 'eyeball to eyeball with the whole world'.[30] This visual linking of message and medium, that is to say, the person Bergoglio/Francis, reinforces the title of the film, *A Man of His Word*: 'That is exactly what Pope Francis is for me, a man who keeps his word, who practices what he preaches.'[31] In accordance with Francis' style of communication, of expressing his message in personal gestures, Wenders is interested in the content of the message, in this case the Pope's, but wants to take it into the performative medium of images. The film, he says, 'can contribute to changing the images we carry within us and the way we look at the world.' A member of the audience 'can be inspired to find new images of a better world'.[32]

IV Conclusion: Political night prayers today

'Political night prayers' are back, in our time and in our societies. People prayed for democracy in Cologne in 2017 using more or less this slogan, as the conference of the extreme right-wing AFD party was taking place.[33] In January 2019 an 'Inter-Religious Political Night Prayer' took place in Salzburg.[34] Earlier, in December 2018, in Linz, also in Austria, Political Prayer took place for the first time under the slogan 'Together for Democracy and Humanity', combining solidarity with refugees with concern for social cohesion and welfare provision.[35] As we see, political night prayers combine the perspectives of cultural and material solidarity, both of which form the foundations of an open, democratic society. In the context of such liturgical acts, however, this solidarity is not just called for in speech, but also to some extent performed, represented and put into practice, at least in the ecumenical and inter-religious organisation of the events. The political night prayers display and bring about what they stand for: unity despite difference. And they combine this content and this dramatic presentation with the foundations of the Christian faith.

So political night prayers are back. Bearing in mind the significance of an understanding of the public sphere as having socio-economic and participatory dimensions (Fraser) and in terms of performance (Alexander), we can see their relevance. In the wake of Francis' public political option for the poor, which he is able to combine with (faith) symbols and communicate, they also deserve a theological welcome.

Translated by Francis McDonagh

Notes

1. This article is based on a (longer) lecture given at the Faculty Day of the faculty of Catholic theology at the University of Innsbruck entitled 'Not of this World. Religion in the Public Sphere', 21 May 2019.
2. On the eventful year 1968, see, for example, Sebastian Holzbrecher et al. (ed.), *Revolte in der Kirche? Das Jahr 1968 und seine Folgen in der Kirche* (Freiburg 2018); Peter Neuner, Turbulenter Aufbruch. *Die 60er Jahre zwischen Konzil und konservativer Wende* (Freiburg 2019).
3. For the original details and further references, see: https://www.dorothee-soelle.de/über-dorothee-sölle/politisches-nachtgebet/ (accessed 10.05.2020), and Peter Neuner, *Turbulenter Aufbruch*, pp 146–152.
4. Dorothee Sölle, *Political Theology* (Philadelphia, PA, 1974). Sölle writes that the book would have been 'unthinkable without the many conversations with friends from the Cologne Political Night Prayers Working Group' (p.10). The book also contains examples of three political night prayers (pp 111-183). There are also source references with comments from Sölle (pp 221-222). Translations and page references from the German edition, *Politische Theologie* (Stuttgart, 1982).
5. Sölle, *Politische Theologie*, p. 13. There is a similar argument (also based on the Enlightenment) in Johann Baptist Metz, *Zur Theologie der Welt*, Mainz and Munich, 1969, p. 103. [English translation: *Theology of the World* (New York, 1969).
6. Sölle, *Politische Theologie*, p. 139.
7. See also the instructive survey by Edmund Arens, 'Going public. Öffentliche Religionen und Öffentliche Theologie', in: Arens et al. (ed.), *Integrationspotenziale von Religion und Zivilgesellschaft. Theoretische und empirische Befunde* (Zürich, 2016), pp 19–69. In relation to public religion and public theology, Arens distinguishes four conceptions of the public sphere: the discursive, in the media, performative and politically organised. In this article I would like to use the specific example of (historic and current) political night prayers to highlight particularly the performative dimension of the public sphere and significance of socio- economic conditions for a political theology in the public sphere.
8. On the idea of a deliberative democracy in Habermas see the overview in Walter Reese-Schäfer, *Jürgen Habermas*, (Frankfurt am Main, 2001), pp 91–117.
9. Florian Höhne, *Öffentliche Theologie. Begriffsgeschichte und Grundfragen* (Leipzig, 2015), p. 48.
10. Jürgen Habermas, *Faktizität und Geltung. Beiträge zur Diskurstheorie des Rechts und des demokratischen Rechtsstaats* (Frankfurt am Main, 2017), p. 430. English edition: *Between Facts and Norms,* Cambridge, MA, and London, 1996.
11. Habermas, *Faktizität und Geltung. Beiträge zur Diskurstheorie des Rechts und des demokratischen Rechtsstaats*, p. 430.
12. Habermas, *Faktizität und Geltung*, p. 443.
13. *Faktizität und Geltung*, p. 443.
14. *Faktizität und Geltung*, pp 430-431.
15. Nancy Fraser, *Die halbierte Gerechtigkeit. Schlüsselbegriffe des postindustriellen Sozialstaats* (Frankfurt am Main, 2001), p. 122. [Original edition: *Justice Interruptus: Critical Reflections on the 'Postsocialist' Condition* (New York, 1997)]
16. Nancy Fraser, *Die halbierte Gerechtigkeit. Schlüsselbegriffe des postindustriellen*

Sozialstaats, p. 127. On the continuing validity of Fraser's critique of liberal concepts of the public sphere such as Habermas's, see Michael Reder, 'Öffentlichkeit und Liberalismus. Eine pragmatische Neubestimmung anhand des Verhältnisses von Öffentlichkeit und Religion', in: Judith Könemann and Saskia Wendel (ed.), *Religion, Öffentlichkeit, Moderne. Transdisziplinäre Perspektiven* (Bielefeld,2016), pp 227–256, quotation from p. 232.

17. See Jeffrey C. Alexander, *The Civil Sphere*, New York 2006; for a useful summary of Alexander's model, see Arens, 'Going public. Öffentliche Religionen und Öffentliche Theologie', pp 24-26. I have discussed the performative dimension of what are also public inter-religious dialogues in: Ansgar Kreutzer, 'Die Performanz des interreligiösen Dialogs für die plurale Gesellschaft – und ihre theologische Bedeutung', in: Ansgar Kreutzer et al. (ed.), *Vielfalt zeigen. Religion, Konfession und Kultur in Vermittlung* [Festschrift F.-J. Bäumer] (Ostfildern, 2019), pp 119–141.

18. Alexander, *The Civil Sphere*, p. 250. [Translation from the German]

19. This is Arens' description of Alexander's position: Arens, *Going Public*, pp 25-26.

20. The theological literature on the current Pope is already extensive; see, for example, the multi-faceted special issue *Phänomen Franziskus, Theologisch-praktische Quartalschrift* 163/1 (2015), which also discusses Pope Francis's impact on the public sphere. For a political and social profile of Francis, see Norbert Mette, *Nicht gleichgültig bleiben! Die soziale Botschaft von Papst Franziskus* (Ostfildern, 2017).

21. Pope Francis, *Apostolic Exhortation Evangelii Gaudium: On the Proclamation of the Gospel in Today's World*, Rome, 24 November 2013, 183: http://www.vatican.va/content/francesco/en/apost_exhortations/documents/papa-francesco_esortazione-ap_20131124_evangelii-gaudium.html

22. Mette, *Nicht gleichgültig bleiben!*, p. 94.

23. See Ansgar Kreutzer, 'Option für die Armen. Theologische Sensibilität für Ausgeschlossene', in: Kreutzer, *Politische Theologie für heute. Aktualisierungen und Konkretionen eines theologischen Programms* (Freiburg, 2017), pp 144–162.

24. Jürgen Werbick, *Kleine Gotteslehre im Dialog mit Papst Franziskus* (Freiburg, 2018), p. 18.

25. Francis, Address to the Participants in the First World Meeting of Popular Movements, Rome, 28 October 2014: http://w2.vatican.va/content/francesco/en/speeches/2014/october/documents/papa-francesco_20141028_incontro-mondiale-movimenti-popolari.html

26. Mette, *Nicht gleichgültig bleiben!*, p. 96.

27. On Francis' sensitivity to symbols, see Kreutzer, *Option für die Armen*, pp 151, 158.

28. See Wim Wenders, *Papst Franziskus. Ein Mann seines Wortes. Transkript des Films*, Hamburg 2018, a booklet accompanying a DVD.

29. See the interview Wenders gave about his intentions, which is included in the booklet accompanying the DVD, pp 40-48.

30. Wenders, DVD booklet, pp 43, 42.

31. DVD booklet, p. 44.

32. DVD booklet, p. 47.

33. See https://www.domradio.de/themen/kirche-und-politik/2017-04-22/christen-setzen-politisches-nachtgebet-gegen-afd-parteitag (Accessed 11.05.2020).

34. See https://www.facebook.com/PolitischesNachtgebetSalzburg/videos/vb.348427009321790/2048507121870231/?type=2&theater (Accessed 11.05.2020).

35. See https://www.dioezese-linz.at/politisches-gebet-gemeinsam-fuer-demokratie-und-menschlichkeit (Accessed 11.05.2020).

Theology and the Power of Liberation

FRANCISCO DE AQUINO JÚNIOR

As intellectus fidei, *theology is constituted as an intellectualisation of a faith that consists of a sharing in and a collaboration with God's salvational and liberational purposes for humanity and also of being at the intellectual and critical service of its historical dynamic. It is this visceral linkage with a liberational faith (faith and liberation), which makes theology a power for liberation connected to the broadest range of historic powers and dynamics of liberation (theology and liberation). Through this linkage, theology's intellectual specificity and essence of being a moment of faith are simultaneously affirmed.*

I Introduction

Theology is the "*intellectus fidei*"[1] and, as such is inseparable from faith: it is both a moment within faith (an intellectual dimension) and is at the service of faith (a socio-ecclesiastical dimension). To the extent that faith consists in entrusting oneself to God and to building a life in accordance with his approach and also to the extent that God reveals himself as a liberating saviour, then faith has a dynamic quality of liberation and salvation: A liberational God demands a liberational faith. And it is this quality that bestows on theology, in its sense of *intellectus fidei*, the dynamic qualities of liberation and salvation in the double sense of both the *intelligence* of a liberational faith and of being at the *service* of a liberational faith. However irreducible it might be as an intellectual activity, the power of liberation theology is inseparable from the power of the liberation of faith. Hence the unbreakable chain: God the liberator – liberational faith – liberational theology.

II Faith and Liberation

In as much as it consists of entrusting oneself to God and of shaping one's life through its inherent energy and propensity to humanity, faith is constitutively referenced, determined and configured by how God both is and acts. God is shown through the history of Israel and the life of Jesus of Nazareth as being both present and active in history (no matter how transcendent He is: He is *within* and not *of* history) and on the side of the poor and the marginalised: poor, orphaned, widowed, outsider.... (no matter how universal in his love and as a saviour). This is his most fundamental quality or characteristic – to the extent of being identified and known as the God of liberation and as the God of the poor and the marginalised.[2]

Indeed, God manifested himself in Israel and in Jesus of Nazareth as a God who was on the side of the poor and the marginalised (Cf. John 9,11), to the point of identifying himself with them (Cf. Matthew 25, 31-46). As Jon Sobrino has always insisted, "the relationship of God with the poor of this world appears as a constant within his revelation...[ ], it is not only conjunctural and transitory, but structural. A transcendental correlation exists between the revelation of God and the clamouring of the poor".[3] This is an integral component of the revelation, something that speaks to the deepest of God's Mysteries. To be revealed through the liberational process of Exodus (and not through Pharaonic domination) and by Jesus' liberational praxis (and not through the domineering praxis of Caesar) is not a mere point of detail, a happen-stance or a dressing up, but something essential, something that has to do with the very Mystery of a God who cannot assume the "form" of a Pharaoh or a Caesar (tyrannical) without denying his very self (Liberator – Father).

And He continues to act across history through his Spirit: the Spirit through which all things were created; the Spirit that spoke and acted through the prophets and popular wisdom; the Spirit that anointed, guided and sustained Jesus in his mission of telling the Good News to the poor (Luke 4, 18; Acts 10, 38). Not by chance is the Spirit invoked in the Church, in ancient hymns such as "Father of the poor". Latin American pneumatological studies[4] have consistently emphasised that, "the Spirit of the Lord acts from the bottom up", to use an expression much loved by Victor Codina.

This way of God's being and behaving is a determinant of faith. If faith is a trusting and faithful adherence to the God who has revealed himself through the history of Israel and in the life and praxis of Jesus, it is thus constitutively referenced and shaped by God in the manner of this being and behaving. Christian faith can only be understood from a standpoint of the God of Israel and Jesus. It is the faith in a God who is the liberator of the poor and marginalised which both implies and becomes real through active engagement in salvation and liberation. While it cannot be reduced to this alone, it remains one of its most basic emblems or characteristics. As Pope Francis has affirmed, "there exists an indissoluble link between our faith and the poor".[5] It is really not possible to speak of Christian faith without the dynamic of liberation and salvation. This is where we understand the prophetic insistence of Sobrino that "there is no salvation other than for the poor".[6]

In this respect, faith is configured as a way of life that brings the power and dynamic of liberation to the poor and the marginalised: be it through the denouncing of various forms of injustice and oppression, be it through the defence of their rights. It is the liberational character or dimension of faith that, in some way, connects – by strengthening, justifying, purifying and/or extending – with broadest range of liberation movements across history.

It is true that Christians have not always followed up on this and have even manipulated, perverted and turned away from this way of life, taking on and reinforcing historical approaches to domination and oppression. The truth of this can be seen both in Holy Scripture and throughout the history of Christianity. And it is still very much there today. You just have to consider the way in which extreme right wing governments in Latin America, in the US and Europe identify themselves as "Christian" and as defenders of the "Christian tradition", using "religion" to justify their neo-liberal economic policies, their aversion to human rights, their wide range of prejudice and racism and even the character and practice of the fascist and/or Nazi approach. The present Brazilian government is the clearest and most transparent example of the perversion and manipulation of the Christian faith: "Brazil above everything; God above us all" and as for the poor, the afro-brazilians, the homosexuals, the imprisoned and so on, let them die. And the most scandalous thing about this is that it happens with the support and complicity of a broad part of the Church and its ministers...

But let us not forget that this manipulation and perversion of faith has always been denounced and fought against as idolatry by prophecy and the wisdom of Israel. (Cf. Isaiah 10,1-2; Ecclesiastes 34, 24-26).[7] Jesus fits into this tradition of sapient and prophetic defence of the poor and the marginalised: he announces the Good News of the Kingdom of God to the poor (Cf. Luke 4, 18-19; Luke 6, 20-26; Matthew 5, 1-12), he uses the cause of the poor as a criterion and as a scatological approach (Cf. Luke 10, 25-27; Matthew 25, 3-46) and, *because of this*, is crucified and resurrected (Cf. Corinthians 2, 9-11; Acts 10, 36-43). And, within His tradition we find all of those who take up the cause of the poor and the marginalised, who defend and fight for their rights, even to the point of martyrdom such as Oscar Romero and so many other men and women who have given their lives for the cause of the poor... They unmasked and denounced the perversion and misuse of faith by those groups and their associates that dominated society; they re-energised and brought life faithfully and creatively to the potential of faith to bring liberation and salvation, strengthening the historical approach of liberation, always based around the needs and the rights of the poor and the marginalised.[8]

III Theology and Liberation

It is the quality and/or dynamism of faith that in the end both enables and makes a necessity of a theology of liberation both supporting and strengthening historical processes of liberation. Obviously, a faith of liberation does not automatically lead to a theology of liberation. The theological practice has its own specificities and its furthering requires wisdom, knowledge, customs, methods and so on, all of which confer a certain degree of autonomy and irreducibility. Nevertheless, in as much as being *intellectus fidei*, theology in practice is an instant of faith which gives it its ultimate epistemological and theological resolve. Therefore, whilst a faith of liberation does not automatically give rise to a theology of liberation, only a faith of liberation both enables and makes a necessity of such a theology.[9]

In speaking of liberation theology, we are speaking of a theology that is directly constituted as an intellectualisation of a liberational faith (intellectual dimension) and as something which intellectually is at the service of that same faith (ecclesiastical dimension) and, indirectly, through faith, of the widest range of historical processes of liberation (social dimension). This guarantees both the intellectual specificity of the theology and its present qualities of ecclesiastical and a wider societal praxis.

IV The faith moment

It is the liberational quality/dynamic of faith, as a way of life, that is to say, actions/praxis, that ultimately confer on theology – *intellectus fidei* – the same qualities. However advanced, progressive or revolutionary a theology might be, if it is not linked to dynamic or real processes of liberation it will never get beyond the stage of ineffectual theory. This is the academic risk for progressive theologians and theological methods: theologies without: "the smell of the people and the street" as Pope Francis has said;[10] "docetistic" theologians, as would Jon Sobrino say.[11] Only in so far as it arises from and is the product of concrete liberational steps and /or is adopted in such steps can a theology be constituted as a power for liberation that encourages authentic liberational processes both critically and constructively. What Ignacio Ellacuria said of philosophy , is equally applicable, *mutatis mutandis*, to theology: It can only play a liberational role if it is viscerally joined to a liberational praxis.

Latin American theology[13] is a very clear example of one constituted as a liberating and/or liberation theology precisely through being viscerally linked to lives through the processes of liberation. We know that in and of itself it is not sufficient to bring about liberation and thus has never been reduced to a mere "religion of deliverance" (Juan Luis Segundo). It can be understood as a moment in the process through which the world is transformed, opening itself [.....] to the Kingdom of God and, as such, as a "theology of liberation" (Gustavo Gutiérrez).[14] We should not be talking about a theology of liberation without also talking of the historic processes of liberation of the country people, the native Indians, working people, women, the homeless, the victims of agri-hydro business, neighbourhood struggles, LGBT communities and so on. What belongs to this theology, these theologies, is making explicit the dimensions of salvation and spirituality inherent in these liberational processes, such that they be comprehended and lived by Christians as both a dimension and a necessary requirement of their faith.

V The intellectual moment

The fact of being a moment of faith lived in and in accordance with liberational processes in no way comprises the intellectual specificity and character of this theology in the dual sense of both being an "intellectualisation of faith" and "at the intellectual service of faith".

In as much as it is an *intellectualisation of faith*, theology is only possible within the broadest context of faith. You cannot have theology without faith, in spite of faith and far less, set against faith. Something quite distinct is a critical reflection on faith with its processes of reductionism, manipulation and even perversion, to the point where faith becomes a dynamic power of domination and, as such, a practical negation of God and of his liberation and salvational design for humanity. But such a criticism is only possible within the prophetic-sapient tradition of Israel and of Jesus Christ, from which standpoint the manipulation and perversion can be seen for what they are. And, here, working theology implies and requires both a very broad and deep approach to be taken of Christian tradition with its first references and permanent "canon" law contained in Sacred Scripture, and great lucidity and criticality with regard to the historic processes of living in faith and the possible/actual exploitation and perversion both in past and the present day.

In being *at the intellectual service of faith*, theology has a function that is both critical and creative in the broadest sense of living with faith. Critical, as much in the sense of being linked to any form of reductionism of faith, as with regard to the widest kinds of exploitation and perversion of faith within the Church and society and also with regard to the broadest sense of historical societal processes to the extent that they shaped themselves beyond any intentional ecclesiastical sense of ownership or avowal, as a negation (sin) or as a mediation (salvation) of God's purposes of liberation and salvation for humanity. Creative, in the sense of helping Christians to discern God's purposes and calls in those situations or contexts where they found themselves and assumed with creative faithfulness this or that purpose or call, seeking and necessary means and intermediation, notwithstanding their limits and ambiguities.

It is this critical and creative character that makes theology, as *intellectus fidei* or as an intellectual moment of faith, a power for liberation that favours and strengthens historical processes of liberation. Decoupled from a faith that is both salvational and liberational, theology " even more than weakening necessary theological praxis, ceases to be an *intellectus fidei*, becoming a study of inoperabilities".[15]

VI Conclusion

If theology wishes to be consistent with the intellectual character (*intellectus*) of salvational and liberational faith (*fidei*), it must be viscerally tied to this faith in the dual sense of intellectualisation and of being at its service both critically and creatively and, so can be constituted as a force for liberation in the world.

The constant risk and temptation for theology is to close in on itself, to build theories upon theories, to create a world apart, ceasing to be both the intellectualisation of faith and at its service. Hence Pope Francis' warning to "avoid a theology which exhausts itself in academic arguments, regarding humanity [from] an ivory tower". Theology, he says, must be, "sited and founded in Revelation, in Tradition", but must "also" be part of the "social and cultural processes" that we experience in "the Church" and in the "world". We should not be satisfied with a, "theology of the office". The place for theology is at the "frontiers" of life. "Good theologians, like good shepherds, have the smell of the people and the street, and like them, pour oil and wine on mankind's wounds". The theologian needed by the Church and the world is not a "museum theology gathering facts and information about the revelation without, despite all of this, really knowing what to do with them, nor a spectator of history". The theologian should be "someone who is really capable of building humanity around him/her, of transmitting the divine Christian truth in ways that are truly human and not be a talentless intellectual, an ethicist without kindness nor a bureaucrat of the sacred".[16] It should not happen that theologians, absorbed by their research and academic debates, pass by on the other side of our Lord who has fallen by the way. It is important that theology is placed at the intellectual service of a faith that is lived in participation and in collaboration with the God's purposes of salvation and liberation for humanity and that it holds the poor and the marginalised as the focus of its scatological measures and criteria. (Matthew 25, 31-46)

Translated by Christopher Lawrence

Notes

1. *Intellectus fidei* – Understanding of faith
2. Cf. Jorge Pixley, *A história de Israel a partir dos pobres*, Petrópolis: Vozes, 2002; Rinaldo Fabris, A opção pelos pobres na Bíblia, São Paulo: Paulinas, 1991; Gustavo Gutiérrez, *O Deus da vida*, São Paulo: Loyola, 1992; Ronaldo Muñoz, O Deus dos cristãos, Petrópolis: Vozes, 1989; Idem., *Trindade de Deus Amor oferecido em Jesus, o Cristo*, São Paulo: Paulinas, 2002.
3. Jon Sobrino, "Teología en un mundo sufriente. La teología de la liberación como 'intellectus amoris'", em: Idem., *El principio–misericordia. Bajar de la cruz a los pueblos crucificados*, Santander: Sal Terrae, 1992, 47-80, 55.
4. Cf. Jorge Pixley, *Vida no espírito. O projeto messiânico de Jesus depois da ressureição*, Petrópolis: Vozes, 1997; Victor Codina, *Creio no Espírito Santo. Pneumatologia narrativa*, São Paulo: Paulinas, 1997; Idem., "Não extingais o Espírito" (1Ts 1, 19): Iniciação à pneumatologia, São Paulo: Paulinas, 2010; Idem., *El Espíritu del Señor actua desde abajo*, Santander: Sal Terrae, 2015; José Comblin, *O Espírito Santo e a Tradição de Jesus. Obra póstuma*, São Bernardo do Campo: Nhanduti, 2012; Leonardo Boff, *O Espírito Santo: Fogo interior, doador de vida e Pai dos pobres*, Petrópolis: Vozes, 2013.
5. Papa Francisco, *Exortação Apostólica Evangelii Gaudium: Sobre o anúncio do Evangelho no mundo atual*, São Paulo: Paulinas, 48.
6. Cf. Jon Sobrino, *Fuera de los pobres no hay salvación. Pequeños ensayos utópico-proféticos*, Madrid: Trotta, 2007.
7. Cf. Gustavo Gutiérrez, *O Deus da vida*, São Paulo: Loyola, 1992, 75-93.
8. Cf. Francisco de Aquino Júnior. *Organizações populares*, São Paulo: Paulinas, 2018.
9. Cf. Ignacio Ellacuría, "La teología como momento ideológico de la praxis eclesial", *Escritos Teológicos* I. San Salvador: UCA, 2000, 163-185; Idem., "Relación teoría y praxis en la teología de la liberación", *Escritos Teológicos* I, San Salvador: UCA, 2000, 235-245; Francisco de Aquino Júnior, *Teoria Teológica – Práxis Teologal: Sobre o método da Teologia da Libertação*, São Paulo: Paulinas, 2012.
10. Cf. Papa Francisco. *Carta ao Cardeal de Buenos Aires por ocasião dos cem anos da Faculdade de Teologia da Universidade Católica Argentina*, A Santa Sé, Vaticano, 3 de Março de 2015, em http://w2.vatican.va/content/francesco/pt/letters/2015/documents/papa-francesco_20150303_lettera-universita-cattolica-argentina.html [23.12.2019].
11. Cf. Jon Sobrino, "Teología desde la realidad", em: Susin, Luiz Carlos (org.). *O Mar se abriu: Trinta anos de teologia na América Latina*, São Paulo: Loyola, 2000, 153-170, 168.
12. Cf. Ignacio Ellacuría, "Función liberadora de la filosofía", *Escritos Políticos* I, San Salvador: UCA, 1993, 93-121.
13. Cf. Francisco de Aquino Júnior, "Questões fundamentais de teologia da libertação".

Perspectiva Teológica 48 (2016) 245-268.
14. Gustavo Gutiérrez, *Teologia da Libertação: Perspectivas*, São Paulo: Loyola, 2000, 74.
15. Ignacio Ellacuría, "Relación teoría y praxis en la teología de la liberación", *Escritos Teológicos* I, San Salvador: UCA, 2000, 235-245, 241s.
16. Papa Francisco. *Carta ao Cardeal de Buenos Aires por ocasião dos cem anos da Faculdade de Teologia da Universidade Católica Argentina*, A Santa Sé, Vaticano, 3 de Março de 2015, em http://w2.vatican.va/content/francesco/pt/letters/2015/documents/papa-francesco_20150303_lettera-universita-cattolica-argentina.html [23.12.2019].

Protesting Patriarchal Power: The Task of Political Theology in Creating Solidarity and Sustaining Activism

TANYA VAN WYK

There is a global increase in protest movements focussed on the lives of women. These include protests against a lack of representation, protests about the pay-gap and very prominent protests against gender-based violence and sexual harassment. Some of these protest movements go as far back as 25 years, including awareness campaigns about gender-based violence and empowerment of women organised by the United Nations and the World Council of Churches. Yet, change is slow and often not forthcoming and there is an increase in gender-based violence. The common denominator is entrenched power. The essay explores the way in which political theology reacts to power and how it can contribute to concerted activism, which is needed to make a lasting change. It is suggested that political theology could be helpful to shift from oppressive power to a collective resistance.

I Responding to contexts? Political theology and its task today

In an article I wrote a few years ago,[1] I argued that political theology is a critical theology, and that it is a theology with its face turned toward the world. I had learned this from Johann Baptist-Metz and Jürgen Moltmann, who count amongst the theologians who influenced me profoundly with regard to the articulation of my own understanding of political theology.

When I wrote about it initially, I understood political theology in its broadest sense, namely as a hermeneutics of suspicion (as coined by Paul Ricoeur) with regard to power and its' influence in the Christian church and Christian theology, which together constitute my main contexts. I maintain that departure point. Gradual experience of my contexts, however, has led me to the realisation that these contexts are profoundly influenced by a single facet of my existential existence, namely my gender: I am a woman. Therefore I am not merely part of the Christian church and I am not merely a theologian, I am first and foremost a *woman* that is part of the Christian church and I am a *woman* theologian. Being a woman in an ecclesial and theological context determines your experiences of that context in a profound and continuous way. Being a woman within those contexts within the broader South African context with one of the highest rates of gender-based violence and femicide in the world, further compounds and determines that experience. It is not an 'add-on' identity marker of my existence – it is the determining one. This has had a profound influence on my political theology and the way I characterise its content and purpose. Therefore, if I could make a more nuanced and focussed suggestion today towards the content and task of political theology I would probably argue that there is no such thing as a political theology, rather there are multiple political theologies, which are shaped by the context from which they emanate. Context shapes the questions and methodologies of political theology. This short essay is an attempt of reflecting on the possible contribution and/or tasks of political theology as response to the simultaneous increase of protest movements against gender-based violence and an increase in the violence itself.

II Gender-based violence: agency, activism and solidarity

> Women are dying, not because we don't know how to save them. They're dying because we have yet to decide they're worth saving. And as a man, I am ashamed.[2]

At the time of writing this essay, the 2019 United Nations' 16 days of activism against gender-based violence has commenced. This year it is aligned to both the UN's UNiTE campaign[3] to end violence against women by 2030 and the UN Women's Generation Equality campaign that marks the 25th anniversary of the Beijing declaration and platform of actions that was established at the UN's 4th World Conference on Women: Action for Equality, Development and Peace in 1995.

That is a mouthful. Or a 'bucket load' of campaigns aimed at addressing the global pandemic of violence against women that is based on the persistent devaluing of women's lives: #MeToo, #Time'sUp, #TheTotalShutdown and the 'Am I next?'-protests. During 2017-2019 movements and campaigns organised by civil society, aimed at gender equality and protest against gender-based violence, have certainly gained momentum. Amid this, the Thursdays-in-Black movement initiated by the World Council of Churches (WCC) during the 'Decade of Churches in solidarity with Women' (1988-1998), has also received sustained attention.

The momentum that these campaigns generate is a welcome turn of events. However, if both the UN and the WCC initiated formal protest and awareness campaigns more or less 25 years ago, what has the impact of these campaigns been in light of statistics that point to an increase in gender-based violence against women?[4] Two and a half decades is a long time for there to be only a slight to no difference in the lives of millions of women.

In response to this question, it is alarming to note that there is a simultaneous phenomenon: there is an increase in gender-based violence and there is an increase in protest campaigns. Not that the campaigns themselves are to be blamed, rather the increase in awareness and protest with regard to the situations of women globally coincides with the emergence of debates about the marginalisation of men (which has happened in my own ecclesial context) are. It seems the protests are symbols of a growing threat to existing structures of power, be it power in relationships, knowledge-construction and leadership. This threat of diminishing power leads to increased violence. The decade after the end of apartheid in South Africa serves as an example. As Romi Sigsworth and Nahla Vlaji[5] have indicated, sexual and gender-based violence against women increased after the end of apartheid, because the violence is informed by pre-conflict power relations. 'Pre-existing gendered hierarchies and patriarchal norms which inform the dominant forms of masculinity in pre-conflict settings, can run up against shifting gender roles and identities during the conflict, as well as new values of gender equality introduced during the transition'.[6] Violence against women is an assertion of power or a desire to keep power. There are different forms of violence in this regard: physical and emotional violence, as well as political, social and economic violence. The type of violence is related to the type of power that is under threat, because gender is embedded in relations of having power or being without.[7]

In the decade after the formal end of apartheid, Graeme Simpson and Gerald Kraak (1998) provided an analysis of the link between a loss of power and increased violence against women in South Africa:

> Given the enduring tradition and history of patriarchal society, in which men have been accustomed to political and economic power, and the more recent realities of political and social change in which they feel a loss of power and control, violence has become an important vehicle for re-asserting their masculine identity and influence. This is true of family killings in white middle-class Afrikaner society – where political and social changes have eroded the traditional power base of Afrikaner men – as it is in black working class society – where unemployment may be experienced in exactly the same way. Economic and political changes are fundamentally undermining the identities conferred upon men by patriarchy ...men as bread-winners ... as guardians ...as protectors. They must seek alternative vehicles for sustaining a sense of self and identity. And violence is such a vehicle.

In April 2019 the results of the first gender survey to be conducted in South Africa was released.[8] It was reported that culture, traditional practices and customary law influenced gender attitudes which are contrary to gender equality. The study illustrated that there is a significant gender gap regarding attitudes about employment, but there is a much smaller gender gap with regard to certain cultural aspects. Some of the results include:

- When jobs are scarce, men have more right to work than women (41% men; 28% women agreed)
- Women should listen and obey when traditional leaders speak (85% men; 71% women agreed)
- In your culture, a woman should listen to her husband (85% men; 82%

women agreed)
• Women should take their husband's last name when they get married (85% men; 78% women agreed)
• Women who know their place will not get beaten (60% men; 52% women agreed)

Religious contexts are not exempt from the phenomenon that growing awareness and focus on gender equality leads to resolute resistance that result in different forms of violence. It accounts for the dynamics I recently witnessed at the general assembly of my church denomination, the Netherdutch Reformed Church (NRCA). This year (2019) marks 40 years since the NRCA allowed women to be ordained as ministers in the church in 1979. During the ensuing four decades a steady stream of women studied theology and were ordained as ministers, even though at present women make up 28% of the entire minister-corps as opposed to 72% men. During the general assembly (held during September 2019), a survey about women's participation and representation in the NRCA was introduced as one of the main discussion points during the assembly.[9] The main purpose of this was to highlight the non-existence of women in leadership positions and the prevalence of sexual harassment and unethical labour practise in the church.

Although the delegates supported the research conducted in the survey, acknowledged and emphasised the importance of the representation of women in all levels of leadership within the church and condemned sexual harassment and violence,[10] the assembled delegates did not elect one single woman minister on the executive council of the general assembly. This is significant, because one woman was part of the previous executive committee. This meant that a purposeful campaign to raise awareness about the lack of female representation amongst ministers and leadership structures in the NRCA coincided with an election in which the presence of female ministers on the executive committee was removed. Coupled with that, sexist language and prejudices about women's ability to lead congregations remained rampant.[11] Transitions in gender and power relations have led to a crisis in masculinity (for the NRCA), as mentioned above. There is an increase in the number of female theological students in the NRCA. This phenomenon occurs in a time where there is a decrease of the institutional church's loss of authority, which leads to dwindling numbers of members and less financial security for ministers. The amount of men enrolling for theological studies with the aim of becoming a minister in the NRCA has decreased significantly[12] to the point where some of the year groups consist of women entirely. Is this a welcome change or is it another indication that women 'may' occupy a position, so long as it does not hold any power? This requires further investigation and is beyond the scope of this essay.

There is of course another reason for the phenomenon that increasing campaigns of protest and awareness with regard to women's lives do not necessarily yield changes for many women around the world. Even though Valentine Moghadam[13] has argued that there is considerably evidence of transnational activism – that is, cross-border collective action in the form of advocacy, it remains a question if women are truly united in protest against the way patriarchy is maintained. With the acknowledgement of the phenomenon of intersectionality – that is, the way different identity markers such as ethnicity, culture, gender, and sexuality intersect to create different epistemologies and paradigms, I sometimes wonder if women are collectively able to reconcile their diversity and work as a collective whole to combat patriarchy. Can the acknowledgment of these differences be a vital power to stimulate uniting across borders, in families, cultures, the church and the workplace? I ask this because there are also women, for ideological, psychological, economic and religious reasons, that view feminist/womanist activists as a threat to what they perceive is a natural, balanced order to the cosmos.[14] This order is based on gender binaries which are expressed in gender roles that are assigned according to an either/or permutation of humanity: either male or female. These women fear marginalisation and in many cases, they fear what was described earlier: a violent reaction to what would be perceived as a challenge to male authority. This is nothing more than a perpetuation of male power and constitutes an unfinished reformation.

III Political theology as resistance to entrenched power
Can political theology help understanding this situation and provide route-markers for a way forward?

In 1970 Carol Hanisch defended the political importance of groups that create awareness. Personal experiences were located within a system of power relationships, Hanisch argued. Her essay titled, 'The Personal is Political', illustrated that you should proverbially always 'take it personal' – if you are a woman – because your experiences as a women are never exempt from power systems that create and maintain knowledge (concepts, ideas and language) that inform and is informed by a complex network of the religious, social, economic and cultural. It means that every experience you will have is informed and shaped by an ideology.

Let me be clear: political theology is not about legitimizing 'the political' in theology, it is about exposing the power of political ideology in theology. That is the first step. Then political theology should ask how theology (religion too) may become involved in civil society movements protesting against dehumanization, and for the purposes of this essay, the dehumanization of women. It is a challenge to reflect on the political function of theology while admitting that Christian religion plays a pervasive role in maintaining patriarchy. As Dorothee Sölle has stated, 'the rules of theological language ... know how to differentiate between the God of the philosophers and the God of Abraham, Isaac and Jacob, [but] are still ignorant of the God of Sarah, Rebecca and Rachel'.[15]

Johann Baptist-Metz once asked, 'is there any such thing as a theological paradigm change independent of reformative processes in the context of the church?'.[16] The political challenge of our time, within the scope of this essay, is a more *concerted* response (particularly by Christian theology and the Christian church) to entrenched gender inequality, the violence that results from it and the power from which it emanates. For this to happen, there needs to be a shift from, what Hannah Pitkin[17][18] described as 'power over' to what Amy Allen described as 'power with'.

It was Hanna Pitkin who coined the terms, 'power over' and 'power to', in the field of political theology.[19] 'Power over' refers to power over other people and the way in which one's own intentions are enforced over the intentions of others.[20] 'Power over' always yields negative results, because it limits the agency of those subjected to it in the forms of domination, oppression and subordination. 'Power to' refers to one's ability to do or achieve something by themselves, independent of others.[21] This power is not about enforcement of power, but rather on the restoration or acknowledgment of the agency to act autonomously. Amy Allen[22] goes further and suggests 'power with' as an approach for collective resistance as well as individual empowerment. In reference to Hanna Arendt, 'power with' is power understood as the human ability to act in concert. Collective power can generate conceptual, normative and psychological resources toward social change.

Protest is both a political and a Christian theological phenomenon. It is political because protests are a critique of the real life results of the mixture of ideology and power. It is theological because at its very heart, Christian faith, as articulated in theology, which is the grammar of faith, is based on the reality that Jesus Christ was crucified as a political and religious rebel. He was crucified because he conveyed a message of reconciliation and restoration to people who were suffering under political, religious and economic oppression. The reality of the intersectionality of women's differing experiences and contexts can become a hurdle to concerted resistance – if it is not situated in the framework of a 'power with' approach. If intersectionality becomes a driving force of reconciling diversity of women across the globe, interlinking protests could become a movement towards a lasting change. It is the task of political theology to remind religion (for this essay – Christian religion) about the havoc created by a power-over approach – even amongst women.

For the price of freedom is constant vigilance.

Bibliography

A. Allen, "Gender and Power", in S.R. Clegg & M. Haugaard (eds.), *The SAGE Handbook of Power*, London: Sage Publications, 2009, 293-310.

G. Göhler, '"Power to" and "Power over"', in S.R. Clegg/ M. Haugaard (eds.), *The SAGE Handbook of Power*, London: Sage Publications, 2009, 28-39.

A. Gouws, *SARChI Chair of Gender Politics: Gender Survey Report*, Stellenbosch: Stellenbosch University, 2019.

C. Hanisch, "The Personal is Political", in S. Firestone/ A. Koedt (eds.), *Notes from the Second Year: Women's Liberation*, New York: Radical Feminist, 1970, 76-77.

E. Kamaara & M. N. Wangila, "Contextual theology and gender

reconstructions in Kenya," *Theologies and Cultures* VI.2 (2009), 110-133.

J.-B. Metz, "Theology in the new paradigm: Political Theology", in W.T. Cavanaugh/ J.W. Bailey & C. Hovey (eds.), *An Eerdmans reader in contemporary political theology*, Grand Rapids. Michigan: Wm. B. Eerdmans Publishing Co., 2012, 316-326.

Valentine M. Moghadam, "Transnational activism", in L.J. Shepard (ed.), *Gender matters in global politics. A feminist introduction to international relations*, New York: Routledge, 2015, 331-346.

C.O.N. Moser, "The gendered continuum of violence and conflict: An operational framework', in C.O.N. Moser & F.C. Clark (eds.), *Victims, perpetrators, or actors: Gender, armed conflict and political violence*, New York: Palgrave Macmillan, 2001, 35-39.

NRCA (Nederduitsch Hervormde Kerk van Afrika), *Agenda van die 72ste Algemene Kerkvergadering/ Agenda of the 72nd General assembly*, 2019a, at https://nhka.org/wp-content/uploads/2019/08/72ste-AKV-agenda.pdf [18 November 2019].

NRCA (Nederduitsch Hervormde Kerk van Afrika), *Konsepnotule/ Minutes of the general assembly*, 2019b, at https://nhka.org/wp-content/uploads/2019/08/72ste-AKV-agenda.pdf [18 November 2019].

H. F. Pitkin, *Wittgenstein and Justice*, Berkeley: University of California Press, 1972.

N. Rao, "Sound Bites", in *TIME Magazine* 194.18 (2019), 56-57.

R. Sigsworth/ N. Valji, "Continuities of violence against women and the limitations of transitional justice", in S. Buckley-Zistel/ R. Stanley (eds.), *Gender in transitional justice*, Hampshire: Palgrave Macmillan, 2012, 115-135.

D. Sölle, "Fatherhood, power and barbarism: Feminist challenges to authoritarian religion", in W.T. Cavanaugh /J.W. Bailey/C. Hovey (eds.), *An Eerdmans reader in contemporary political theology*, Grand Rapids, Michigan: Wm. B. Eerdmans Publishing Co, 2012, 327-336.

E. Van Eck, ''n Vergadering van die vroue, of nie?'/ 'A meeting of women, or not?', *Die Hervormer* 112.8 (2019), 2-3.

T. Van Wyk, 2015, "Political Theology as critical theology", *HTS Theological Studies* 71(3), Art. #3026, 8 pages. http:// dx.doi.org/10.4102/hts. v71i3.3026

Notes

1. T. Van Wyk, 2015, "Political Theology as critical theology", *HTS Theological Studies* 71(3), Art. #3026, 8 pages. http:// dx.doi.org/10.4102/hts. v71i3.3026.
2. N. Rao, 'Sound Bite', *TIME Magazine* 18. (2019), 56-57. Dr Naveen Rao is the senior vice president of the health at the Rockefeller Foundation and he made this remark during a presentation at the TIME 100 Health Summit in October 2019.
3. United Nations Women, 2019, 'UNiTE to end violence against women', accessed at https://www.unwomen.org/en/what-we-do/ending-violence-against-women/take-action/unite on 25 November 2019
4. There is a host of statistics available. For example: http://www.unwomen.org/en/what-we-do/ending-violence-against-women/facts-and-figures; UNFPA (United Nations Population FUND), State of the world population 2019: 'Unfinished business: the pursuit of rights and choices for all', accessible at https://www.unfpa.org/swop-2019; UNICEF, 2017, A Familiar Face: Violence in the lives of children and adolescents; 'South-African Demographic and Health Survey' and 'Crime against women in South Africa', accessible at StatsSA-website; the South-African Human Rights Commission at https://www.sahrc.org.za/index.php/sahrc-media/news/item/1466-gender-based-violence and also SaferSpaces: https://www.saferspaces.org.za/understand/entry/gender-based-violence-in-south-africa.
5. R. Sigsworth/ N. Valji, 'Continuities of violence against women and the limitations of transitional justice', in S. Buckley-Zistel/ R. Stanley (eds.), *Gender in transitional justice*, Hampshire: Palgrave Macmillan, 2012, pp. 115-116.
6. Ibid. p. 117.
7. C.O.N. Moser, "The gendered continuum of violence and conflict: An operational framework', in C.O.N. Moser & F.C. Clark (eds.), *Victims, perpetrators, or actors: Gender, armed conflict and political violence*, New York: Palgrave Macmillan, 2001, 35-39, here 37.
8. A. Gouws, SARChI Chair of Gender Politics, Stellenbosch: Stellenbosch University, 2019.
9. NRCA (Nederduitsch Hervormde Kerk van Afrika), Agenda van die 72ste Algemene Kerkvergadering/ Agenda of the 72nd General assembly, 2019a, pp. 74-78. at https://nhka.org/wp-content/uploads/2019/08/72ste-AKV-agenda.pdf [18 November 2019].
10. NRCA (Nederduitsch Hervormde Kerk van Afrika), Konsepnotule/ Minutes of the general assembly, 2019b, at https://nhka.org/wp-content/uploads/2019/08/72ste-AKV-agenda.pdf [18 November 2019].
11. E. Van Eck, in 'Vergadering van die vroue, of nie?'/ 'A meeting of women, or not?', *Die Hervormer* 8. (2019), p. 3.
12. NRCA (Nederduitsch Hervormde Kerk van Afrika), Agenda van die 72ste Algemene Kerkvergadering/ Agenda of the 72nd General assembly, 2019a, pp. 269-281. at https://nhka.org/wp-content/uploads/2019/08/72ste-AKV-agenda.pdf [18 November 2019].
13. Valentine M. Moghadam, "Transnational activism", in L.J. Shepard (ed.), *Gender matters in global politics. A feminist introduction to international relations*, New York: Routledge, 2015, 331-346.
14. E. Kamaara & M. N. Wangila, Contextual theology and gender reconstructions in Kenya, *Theologies and Cultures* VI.2 (2009), 131.
15. D. Sölle,'Fatherhood, power and barbarism: Feminist challenges to authoritarian

religio', in W.T. Cavanaugh /J.W. Bailey/C. Hovey (eds.), *An Eerdmans reader in contemporary political theology*, Grand Rapids, Michigan: Wm. B. Eerdmans Publishing Co, 2012, p. 327.
16. J.-B. Metz, 'Theology in the new paradigm: Political Theology', in W.T. Cavanaugh/ J.W. Bailey & C. Hovey (eds.), *An Eerdmans reader in contemporary political theology*, Grand Rapids. Michigan: Wm. B. Eerdmans Publishing Co., 2012, p.317.
17. G. Göhler, '"Power to" and "Power over"', in S.R. Clegg/ M. Haugaard (eds.), *The SAGE Handbook of power*, London: Sage Publications, 2009, p. 28.
18. H. F. Pitkin, *Wittgenstein and Justice*, Berkeley: University of California Press, 1972, p. 277.
19. Ibid.
20. G. Göhler, '"Power to" and "Power over"', in S.R. Clegg/ M. Haugaard (eds.), *The SAGE Handbook of Power*, London: Sage Publications, 2009, p. 28.
21. H. F. Pitkin, *Wittgenstein and Justice*, Berkeley: University of California Press, 1972, p. 277.
22. A. Allen, 'Gender and Power', in S.R. Clegg & M. Haugaard (eds.), *The SAGE Handbook of Power*, London: Sage Publications, 2009, p. 295.

Power Dynamics Beyond Collusion and Resistance: "The Catholic Philippines" as Privileged Locus

JOSE MARIO C. FRANCISCO

Filipino Catholicism's social engagement offers a privileged locus for the critical analysis of power dynamics. This engagement has been forged within changing political contexts, including nearly 450 years of colonization, first Spanish and then American, and, since the end of World War II, formal democracy dominated by oligarchy and authoritarian leaders. Catholic groups and individuals among clerics, religious and laity have been often on both sides of political divides, either in collusion with or resistance against the ruling establishment. This essay's critical analysis transcends the collusion-resistance binary relations and provides a thick description of dynamics involving Filipino Catholicism's symbolic, institutional and allied powers. Born out of the interaction between Spanish Catholicism and native culture, the symbolic consists of the network of stories related to Christ's life, revered images and sacred rituals that frame individual and social experience outside of church control. The institutional resides in juridical entities of dioceses and parishes, ministries of religious communities, and church-affiliated lay groups. Often allied with other social actors, the interaction of these powers accounts for the differing forms of Catholicism's social engagement. In the end, three theological insights emerge from this analysis. First, the power dynamics behind social engagement is inclusive and diverse. Second, it underscores the historical yet eschatological nature of engagement. Third, discerning social engagement by all the faithful calls for a multidirectional interplay between the symbolic and the institutional in their specific historical mediations.

The Philippine sociohistorical experience offers a privileged locus for critical analysis of Catholicism's engagement with power. Though recognizing the Gospel's power to transform hearts, this analysis focuses on social engagement in the most populous Catholic nation in Asia. It offers a thick description of power dynamics: first, identifying sources of power and different social engagements, and then discussing related critical theological insights.

I Beyond Collusion and Resistance

Before Western colonialism's entry from the 16th century onward, native settlements, mostly coastal and relatively small except those in Moslem territories, contended with commercial and political powers in the centuries-old Asian maritime trade. Then they became colonized under the Spanish for more than three centuries and the Americans for almost fifty years. Native resistance to these powers were initially escape to the mountains and then armed conflicts — sporadic local revolts, raids from Moslem territories, and the 1896 Philippine Revolution against Spain and the 1899-1902 Philippine-American War. As an American-style constitutional democracy after World War II, the Philippines has been governed by an oligarchy steeped in patronage politics and divided into regional and familial factions. Hence arose governments under "strong leaders": among them, the dictatorial Ferdinand Marcos (1972-1986), the actor Joseph Estrada (1998-2001), and even the current populist Rodrigo Duterte (2016-).[1] Despite "unfinished revolutions" and intermittent reforms under formal democracy, the legacy of this system has been structural poverty of the majority, widening divide between the powerful and the voiceless, and systemic exclusion of constituents such as Muslims, indigenous peoples and women.

Catholicism has had to forge its place in this fractuous landscape. As elsewhere, Filipino Catholics occupy both sides of all political divides. Early Spanish missionaries condemned their accompanying *conquistadores* over treatment of natives. But their 19th century counterparts collaborated with colonial authorities, while Filipino diocesan priests and lay Catholics participated in nationalist and revolutionary movements against Spain and the USA.[2]

Reeling from colonial disestablishment and schisms from the Philippine Independent Church and later *Iglesia ni Cristo*, the Catholic Church felt threatened by church-state separation, American culture and Protestant missions under American governance. In defence, different non-Spanish religious orders established schools and ministries with more modern approaches. American Jesuits and their students organized workers and farmers. Nevertheless, the Catholic Church remained socially conservative, especially during the Cold War era and even after the historic Second Vatican Council (1962-1965) recognized social issues as part of its mission.[3] Catholics continue to be divided. During the Marcos regime, some were supporters while others joined Communist-led groups or the anti-Communist opposition.[4]

Given this divided landscape and differing Catholic reactions, analysing power dynamics through the collusion-or-resistance issue proves inadequate. It is based on the theoretical and practical framework of binary power relations and risks reducing Christian social engagement to ideology. In contrast, this essay proposes a multifaceted approach to the sources of power behind Catholic social engagement.

II The Symbolic Power of Filipino Catholicism

With Catholicism's enduring presence and social engagement, Philippine life and society are marked by a symbolic network of stories related to Christ's life, images of holy women and men, and religious rituals associated with important occasions like harvest season or family bereavement.

Though generated by Spanish Catholicism's missionary efforts, this symbolic network developed with the use of Philippine languages for evangelization and production of religious texts. Despite church concern for fidelity to Catholic Faith and its colonial associations, Catholicism took native form. Native views, values and practices embedded in these languages infiltrated Christian discourse. Moreover, since these texts were used in communal and personal contexts, native appropriation of Catholicism became profoundly rooted.

Even with changing historical contexts during the 20th century, Catholic places of worship, education and other ministries characterize the social landscape. Images of Christ, "Mama Mary" and saints adorn altars at government buildings, homes and vehicles. Traditional religious occasions occupy the yearly calendar: Christmas, the November remembrance of departed relatives, Holy Week and the town patron's feast day.

This symbolic network extends to those not connected to Christian churches. Local sects with eclectic practices abound along traditionally revered mountains or in Metro Manila's urban poor alleys. They often consider leaders like hero Jose Rizal as God's prophet or the Filipino Christ.

Hence this extensive symbolic network wields power beyond church control and shapes religious practice. It offers an array of stories, images and rituals through which people frame their everyday lives. Gemma Tulud Cruz maintains that Filipino migrant workers do not only bring religious objects abroad but also conceive their overseas work in terms of Christian sacrifice.[5]

But this symbolic network's power is most manifest in social engagement. Woven beneath the fabric of everyday life, it irrupts during extraordinary occasions or critical times considered liminal. For instance during and after the colonial periods, social movements tapped into this network. Reynaldo Ileto credits the epic-like *Casaysyan nang Pasiong Mahal* [The Story of the Sacred Passion] (1812) for providing the language for social change among 19th century movements, and Joseph Scalise underscores its communal chanting.[6] John Schumacher locates this network's power in the wider religious tradition "found in the hundreds of different novenas and *devocionarios* ... found in very major Philippine language...[that] did more to form folk religious perceptions, for better or worse, than did the catechism memorized by rote in primary schools."[7]

The January Black Nazarene procession and the popularly-called 1986 EDSA People Power Revolution provide contemporary instances. The whole-day procession of millions from diverse backgrounds along Manila's crowded streets show the public face of religious devotion. The EDSA Revolution against Marcos, though supported by the institutional church and other political forces, made the network's power prominently visible through Catholic images and rituals, so that some piously framed this upheaval as "the exodus of the Filipino people."[8]

Some have considered the extent and power of Filipino Catholicism's symbolic network as nothing more than "cultural Christianity." Such an understanding based on the false dissociation of religion from all other aspects of life proves inadequate in the face of Filipino Catholicism's social engagement.

III The Institutional Power of the Catholic Church

The Philippine Catholic Church's institutional power and footprint follow the official Catholic structure consisting of juridical territories like dioceses and parishes and based on doctrinal beliefs, moral codes and religious practices. It encompasses ministries of religious orders and different lay organizations with varying degrees of church linkages. After Vatican II, other associations like the Catholic Bishops' Conference of the Philippines and the Association of Major Religious Superiors of the Philippines emerged as moral rather than formal juridical entities.

Noteworthy in relation to social engagement is the role of lay groups, non-official juridical entities but missioned to evangelize "the temporal sphere" (*Apostolicam actuositatem* 6). Though traditional organizations like Legion of Mary focus on devotional practices, more recent groups, especially those charismatic or evangelical, have taken differing positions on social issues, often depending on their relations to church leaders. Couples for Christ (CFC) supported the impeachment of President Joseph Ejercito Extrada on corruption charges, while *El Shaddai*, influenced by American prosperity Gospel, supported him.[9]

This institutional footprint involving clerics, religious and laity has extensive reach, especially through strategically located Catholic institutions.[10] It facilitates social engagement by concerted action and moral persuasion, and interaction with the state and other political actors.

In the 1960s, Catholic leaders and groups succeeded in modifying legislation on including Rizal's "anti-Catholic" novels in school curricula, while more recently, they worked with Congress for the Comprehensive Agrarian Reform Law and mobilized parishes and schools against constitutional change.[11]

But less known is how the church's institutional power has supported critics and whistle-blowers against the political establishment. Before the People Power Revolution, religious houses gave refuge to prominent critics including the Commission on Elections staff who refused to encode fraudulent election returns. Since then, whistle-blowers have often approached these communities. Such complex situations have produced either crucial evidence of wrongdoing or tainted and recanted testimonies jeopardizing the church.

However, Filipino Catholicism's institutional power is not monolithic. Though an overwhelming 80% of the total Philippine population identify as Catholic, its hold among its members varies, depending on members' location at church's centre or margins. Thus the church's official voice is not necessarily heeded, as in the issues of the reinstatement of the death penalty or the reproductive health legislation. Related to current President Duterte's war on drugs, this difference between official and popular voices has become most challenging: strong public criticism from some church leaders but overwhelming support from the Catholic majority.

IV Allied Powers of Social and Digital Networks

Filipino Catholicism's symbolic and institutional powers interact with other sources of power in civil society, and thus vary in reach and strength. Unlike contexts like Malaysia where Christian membership, Chinese ethnicity and higher economic status coalesce for greater power, such clear links do not mark Filipino Catholicism.

For example, traditional religions, Islam and Christianity interact across Mindanao, and though some indigenous communities are Muslim or Christian, their "lived religion" is hybrid with elements from these traditions, resulting in either integral development or tension and conflict.

Christian-Buddhist interaction also exemplifies this alliance and hybrid practice. Though local Chinese are traditionally Buddhist, Christians among them continue Buddhist practices. Given Buddhism's non-restrictive borders, such hybridity does not produce inner tension and even promotes cooperation between Christian and Buddhist groups for social engagement. In typhoon Haiyan's aftermath in November 2015, Tzi Chi Foundation, a Taiwan-based Buddhist charity, worked with Catholics and Muslims, even building churches and mosques.[12]

Alliances with other powers on social and digital networks are facilitated by both personal relations and compatibility of visions. Personal relations in Philippine society open doors to influence. Catholic school and parish leaders provide access, albeit informal, to government or civil society power centres. Though these do not necessarily bring support for Catholic social engagement, significant instances show such relations amplifying the Catholic voice.

For example, during the Marcos regime, civil society leaders of FLAG (Free Legal Assistance Group) and NAMFREL (National Movement for Free Election) collaborated with church leaders. In the 1986 presidential election between Marcos and Corazon Aquino, NAMFREL volunteers from Catholic institutions fought massive government fraud; nuns called NAMFREL Marines literally sat on ballot boxes.[13]

Alliances with other Christians and Muslims depend on similarity of social views. The People's Choice Movement, convened in 2015 by Catholic, Protestant and Evangelical laity, protects elections from "guns, goons and gold" and chooses candidates with Christian values.

During the 1990s Mindanao conflict with Moslem factions, Catholic and Protestant bishops and Ulama League of the Philippines members promoted peace through a roving caravan and a million-signature campaign.[14]

With current digital communications, alliances extend into digital space. Catholic groups and individuals create websites and blogs describing their history, vision-mission and activities. But digital alliances wielded greater power in the recent controversy over reproductive health legislation. Lay voices from Catholic schools waged an online campaign criticizing bishops' pastoral letters and galvanizing wider Catholic support for the legislation's passage. Because traditional church communications have been "top-down" from official pronouncements to the pews, digital connectivity has provided a platform for open discussion among Catholics.[15]

This online interaction has currently intensified between supporters and critics of President Duterte's anti-programs like the war on drugs and his anti-Catholic statements. Both sides weaponize digital space through posts and hacking. Duterte's high approval ratings pose a challenge to critical Catholic leaders and laity, and raise questions about Catholicism's symbolic and institutional powers.

V Critical Theological Reflection on Power Dynamics

The thick description of Filipino Catholicism's social engagement sketches its multifaceted power dynamics. Besides indicating collusion or resistance through changing historical instances, it identifies its inherent and allied powers as well as their interactions.

Moreover, it offers a strategic lens for analysing the power dynamics in particular social engagements. Filipino Catholicism wields greater power when all or some of the following conditions obtain: 1) the issue is perceived, consciously or not, as linked to the symbolic network based on salvation history, 2) Catholic positions on the issue do not contradict other social actors' views and interests, 3) the church mobilizes its institutional resources for the issue, and 4) Catholics ally with other actors because of personal relations or similarity of views. These indicate how different sources of power interact and extend the reach and strength of Catholicism's social engagement.[16]

This articulation of power dynamics leads to some theological insights related to Filipino Catholicism's social engagement.

First, the power dynamics involved in Filipino Catholicism's social engagement is inclusive and diverse. It encompasses individuals and groups associated with Catholicism in various ways and interacts with other entities and forces. This inclusive character undermines the often presumed dualism between the religious and the secular, between the spiritual and the temporal as well.

The religious-secular dualism in common theories of secularization has been widely critiqued. Talal Asad insists that such theories lead to an untenable dualism between "a world of self-authenticating things in which we really live as social beings and a religious world that exists only in our imagination."[17] Thus our social world becomes, by definition, that outside the religious.

Official church documents reflects a similar duality between the spiritual and the temporal orders. Though the Vatican II decree *Apostolicam actuositatem* (AA) recognizes the unity of and distinction between both orders and the participation of all in the church's apostolate (AA 5-6), the duality appears in the separation of tasks between clerics and laity: "Pastors have the duty to set forth clearly the principles concerning the purpose of creation and the use to be made of the world, and to provide moral and spiritual helps for the renewal of the temporal order in Christ" while "laymen ought to take on themselves as their distinctive task this renewal of the temporal order, guided by the light of the Gospel and the mind of the Church" (AA 7). While this separation of tasks safeguards the relative autonomy of the temporal and the non-involvement of clerics in public partisan politics, it effectively constitutes the spiritual as the cleric's domain and the temporal as the laity's.

However, Filipino Catholicism's social engagement belies both dualisms. Filipino Catholics, clerics and lay alike, engaged social issues in the spirit of the 1971 Synod document: "action on behalf justice and participation in the transformation of the world fully appear to us as a constitutive dimension of the preaching of the Gospel" ("Justice in the World" 6).

Second, the tensive dynamic between Filipino Catholicism's symbolic and institutional powers uncovers the profound nature of Christian social engagement. This dynamic does not only account for differing social engagements but also underscores its historical yet eschatological nature.

Catholic perspectives often view this dynamic in terms of the charismatic versus the institutional. But such perspectives prove misleading when they ignore the historically mediated character of both powers. On the one hand, Catholicism's symbolic network, far from being an ahistorical spiritual or charismatic core, operates within its living tradition expressed in revered stories, images and rituals. This living tradition constitutes what the 2015 International Theological Commission calls the *sensus fidelium* —"an instinct for the truth of the Gospel, which enables them [all the baptized] to recognize and endorse authentic Christian doctrine and practice, and to reject what is false. That supernatural instinct, intrinsically linked to the gift of faith received in the communion of the Church, is called the *sensus fidei*" ("*Sensus Fidei* in the Life of the Church" 2).

On the other hand, Catholicism's institutional power serves this living tradition expressed in its symbolic network and actualized in particular social engagements. These engagements seek but do not exhaust the fullness of the God's Reign that is yet to come. Thus, they offer what the church discerns as "the least imperfect social arrangement" at that historical moment. This ever provisional character of Catholic social engagement point to what Johann B. Metz calls "the subversive memory of Christian faith."[18]

Third, discerning social engagement by all the faithful then calls for a multidirectional interplay between the symbolic and the institutional in their specific historical mediations. However, Catholic thought tends to consider this as "application" of Catholic social teaching to a particular situation, a deductive process that often pays less attention to the situation's complexity. For instance, the bishops' pastoral letters on Philippine politics, economy and culture, fail to provide coherent social analysis, often resorting to simply identifying "lights and shadows" in Philippine society.[19]

Catholic discernment of social engagement requires a mutual and interactive process that equally respects the living historical tradition of Catholic Faith as well as the "signs of the times" from below. Bradford Hinze's study of the impact of Vatican II on New York parish communities illustrates obedience to God's Word, not only through prophetic proclamations but also in Israel's lamentations. This underlines the singular presence of the Spirit who is the primal origin and accompanying presence of both official teaching and the people's common faith.[20]

These theological insights arising from the power dynamics behind Filipino Catholicism's social engagement invite a more fundamental examination of Christian social engagement as well as its power dynamics. They also suggest the privileged locus of Filipino Catholicism because of its long experience through changing historical contexts and its varied forms of social engagement.

Bibliography

P. N. Abinales, *Images of State Power: Essays on Philippine Politics from the Margins*, Quezon City: University of the Philippines Press, 1998.

P. N. Abinales and Donna J. Amoroso, *State and Society in the Philippines*, 2nd Edition, Quezon City: Ateneo de Manila University Press, 2017.

T. Asad, *Formations of the Secular: Christianity, Islam, Modernity*, Stanford: Stanford University Press, 2003.

C. Barry, The Limits of Conservative Church Reformism in the Democratic Philippines, in: T.-J. Cheng/D. Brown (ed.), *Religious*

Organizations and Democratization: Case Studies from Contemporary Asia, Armonk, NY: M. E. Sharpe, 2006, pp 157–179.

G. T. Cruz, *Into the Deep: A Theological Exploration of the Struggle of the Filipina Domestic Workers in Hong Kong*, Manila: Radboud University Nijmegen, 2006.

A. C. Dy, *Chinese Buddhism in Catholic Philippines: Syncretism as Identity*, Mandaluyong City: Anvil Publishing, 2015.

J. M. C. Francisco, "Facilitating Conditions of Church Power," *Landas*, 24 (2010) no. 1. pp. 137-141.

J. M. C. Francisco, "Mapping Religious and Civil Spaces in Traditional and Charismatic Christianities in the Philippines," *Philippine Studies* 58 Nos. 1-3 (2010), pp. 185-221.

J.M.C. Francisco, "People of God, People of the Nation: Official Catholic Discourse on Nationalism and Nation," *Philippine Studies* 62 Nos. 3-4 (2014), pp. 315-350.

J. M. C. Francisco, "Letting The Texts on RH Speak For Themselves": (Dis)Continuity and (Counter)Point in CBCP Statements," *Philippine Studies* 63 no. 2 (2015), pp. 223-236.

E. M. O. Genilo, "The Catholic Church and the Reproductive Health Bill Debate: The Philippine Experience," *Heythrop Journal* 55 (2014) no. 6, pp. 1052-1065.

B. E. Hinze, *Prophetic Obedience: Ecclesiology for a Dialogical Church*, Maryknoll: Orbis Books, 2016.

R.C. Ileto, *Pasyon and Revolution: Popular Movements in the Philippines*, 1840-1910, Quezon City: Ateneo de Manila University Press, 1979.

J. B. Metz, *Faith in History and Society: Toward a Practical Fundamental Theology*, Trans. David Smith, New York: Seabury Press, 1980.

A F. Moreno, Church, *State, and Civil Society in Postauthoritarian Philippines: Narratives of Engaged Citizenship*, Quezon City: Ateneo de Manila University Press, 2006.

R. Moyer, *Bayan Ko! Images of the Philippine Revolt*, Hongkong: Project 28 Days, 1986.

J. Scalice. Reynaldo, "Ileto's Pasyon and Revolution revisited, a critique", *Sojourn: Journal of Social Issues in Southeeast Asia* 33 (2018) no. 1, pp. 29-58.

J. N. Schumacher, *Readings in Philippine Church History*, Quezon City: Loyola School of Theology, 1982.

J. N. Schumacher, *Revolutionary Clergy*, Quezon City: Ateneo de Manila University Press 1998.

Notes

1. P. N. Abinales and Donna J. Amoroso, *State and Society in the Philippines*, 2nd Edition. Quezon City: Ateneo de Manila University Press, 2017, pp. 311-348.
2. J. N. Schumacher, *Revolutionary Clergy*. Quezon City: Ateneo de Manila University Press 1998.
3. C. Barry, "The Limits of Conservative Church Reformism in the Democratic Philippines", in T.-J. Cheng/D. Brown (ed.), *Religious Organizations and Democratization: Case Studies from Contemporary Asia*, pp. 157–79. Armonk, NY: M. E. Sharpe, 2006.
4. A. F. Moreno, *Church, State, and Civil Society in Postauthoritarian Philippines: Narratives of Engaged Citizenship*, Quezon City: Ateneo de Manila University Press, 2006, pp. 31-68.
5. G. T. Cruz, *Into the Deep: A Theological Exploration of the Struggle of the Filipina Domestic Workers in Hong Kong*, Manila: Radboud University Nijmegen, 2006.
6. R. C. Ileto, *Pasyon and Revolution: Popular Movements in the Philippines, 1840-1910*. Quezon City: Ateneo de Manila University Press, 1979; J. Scalice. "Reynaldo Ileto's Pasyon and Revolution revisited, a critique," *Sojourn: Journal of Social Issues in Southeast Asia* 33 (2018) no. 1, pp. 29-58.
7. J. N. Schumacher, *Readings in Philippine Church History*, Quezon City: Loyola School of Theology, 1982, p. 456.
8. R. Moyer, *Bayan Ko! Images of the Philippine Revolt, Project 28 Days*, Hongkong, 1986.
9. J. M. C. Francisco, "Mapping Religious and Civil Spaces in Traditional and Charismatic Christianities in the Philippines," *Philippine Studies* 58 Nos. 1-3 (2010), pp. 185-221.
10. P. N. Abinales, *Images of State Power: Essays on Philippine Politics from the Margins*. Quezon City: University of the Philippines Press, 1998, pp.166-179.
11. J. M. C. Francisco, "People of God, People of the Nation: Official Catholic Discourse on Nationalism and Nation", *Philippine Studies* 62 Nos. 3-4 (2014), pp. 315-350.
12. A. C. Dy, *Chinese Buddhism in Catholic Philippines: Syncretism as Identity*, Mandaluyong City: Anvil Publishing, 2015, pp. 196-207.
13. A F. Moreno, *Church, State, and Civil Society in Postauthoritarian Philippines: Narratives of Engaged Citizenship*, Quezon City: Ateneo de Manila University Press, 2006, 31-68.
14. Ibid., 110-111.
15. E. M. O. Genilo, "The Catholic Church and the Reproductive Health Bill Debate: The Philippine Experience," *Heythrop Journal* 55 (2014) no. 6, pp. 1052-1065.
16. J. M. C. Francisco, "Facilitating Conditions of Church Power," *Landas*, 24 (2010) no.

1. pp. 137-141.
17. T. Asad, *Formations of the Secular: Christianity, Islam, Modernity*, Stanford: Stanford University Press, 2003, pp. 193-194.
18. J. B. Metz, *Faith in History and Society: Toward a Practical Fundamental Theology*, Trans. David Smith, New York: Seabury Press, 1980, pp. 88-99.
19. J. M. C. Francisco, "People of God, People of the Nation" and "Letting The Texts on RH Speak For Themselves": (Dis)Continuity and (Counter)Point in CBCP Statements," *Philippine Studies* 63 no. 2 (2015), pp. 223-236.
20. B. E. Hinze, *Prophetic Obedience: Ecclesiology for a Dialogical Church*. Maryknoll: Orbis Books, 2016.

Passion Consistent With the Depth of the Wounds of the Oppressed

LA REINE - MARIE MOSELY, S N D

This essay affirms black theology as a survival theology that speaks with passion that is commensurate with the suffering of the oppressed. By juxtaposing two ecclesial meetings in the U.S., one in 1866 and one in 2019, the author describes inattention to the lives of former bondspersons and those of poor and disenfranchised African Americans in Baltimore. Finally, through the lens of synodality, opportunities to journey with unlikely travellers open up and provide the space for the sharing of painful stories so that empathy welcomes truth-telling and all choose to continue the dialogue in truth.

I Introduction

Black liberation theology has much to offer the wider Christian community. J. H. Cone, the father of black theology, displayed throughout his life and his formidable corpus, what it means to acknowledge black experience as an indispensable source when doing theology. He believed that "because black theology is survival theology, *it must speak with a passion consistent with the depths of the wounds of the oppressed.*"[1] The historical record attests to the hatred and injustice levelled against the African American community in the United States and in other regions of the Atlantic slave trade. This same passion has also fuelled the black church. For Cone, the language of theology must be passionate—a "language of commitment, because it is language which seeks to vindicate the afflicted and condemn the enforcers of evil."[2]

Too often, after the killing of unarmed African American men, women, and children by law enforcement, there is no place for black Catholics to go to manage the psychic violence and home-grown terrorism they have known. Catholic religious leaders are either silent or they speak with no passion—some suggesting that they do not wish to incite violence. When they do make comments, they immediately follow them by affirming law enforcement in the very next breath. Cone concludes that 'American theology is racist; it identifies theology as dispassionate analysis of "the tradition," unrelated to the sufferings of the oppressed.'[3]

Moral theologian, B. Massingale has made the broader claim suggesting that "to say that racial injustice is not a major concern of Catholic social teaching would be an understatement".[4] Such a record makes it hard to believe that these leaders have the heart of a shepherd or understand the urgency of the moment for people who are "walking, driving, or studying while black" or for those who are waiting at the southern border seeking safety and a new life. Thankfully, some letters written from individual bishops addressed to their dioceses and archdioceses have been marked by some passion, compassion, hope, and care and tailored to the members of their flock.[5]

In the pages that follow, I will revisit two Catholic ecclesial gatherings that took place in Baltimore, Maryland over a century apart, to observe responses or lack thereof on the part of bishops who are the official teachers of the Catholic faith. Then, I will briefly engage the burgeoning gift of synodality, in the hopes that African American Catholics, God's image in black,[6] can experience a church that can be prophetic, accountable, and fruitful into the 21st century and beyond, especially on behalf of the oppressed.

II The Second Plenary Council of Baltimore, 1866

The year was 1866 when the bishops of the United States gathered for the Second Plenary Council of Baltimore in the country's premier see and first diocese. In Dom Cyprian Davis's magisterial work, *The History of Black Catholics in the United States*, he recounts the circumstances surrounding this plenary council. At the midpoint of the Civil War, Henry Binsse, the Holy See's agent in New York, conveyed to the Congregation of the Propaganda "that it would no longer be possible for the church in the United States to maintain 'a political policy of reticence and abstention.'"[7]

Chattel slavery, after all, rendered bondspersons, property, thus violating all of their human rights. Baltimore Archbishop Martin J. Spalding, reached out to Cardinal Barnabo, the prefect of the Congregation of the Propaganda, a year before the end of the Civil War, and requested that a second plenary council be convoked.[8] One reason Spalding gave for wanting to bring together the U.S. bishops was to discuss a pastoral plan to address the evangelization and the spiritual needs of the soon-to-be-emancipated black Americans.[9] Barnabo gave his approval for this second plenary council and shared Spalding's apostolic concern for this population.[10]

In Spalding's letter to Archbishop McCloskey of New York, informing him of the upcoming council, Spalding referred to the present moment, as "a golden opportunity for reaping a harvest of souls, which neglected may never return."[11] Sadly, the majority of bishops were not open to the pastoral concerns shared by Spalding and Barnabo. Their personal views on the peculiar institution of slavery may have grounded their disinterest. Additionally, these bishops were provoked by the idea that a prefect, who could be made a bishop, would be in charge of this pastoral plan. Nevertheless, Davis notes two examples of bishops who had been in favour of slavery, becoming strong voices in favour of promoting the pastoral care and well-being of formerly enslaved persons.[12] Archbishop Spalding was one such example. Bishop Venot of Savannah was another.[13]

Due to the massive amount of work on the agenda of the Second Plenary Council of Baltimore, the pastoral care of black Americans was relegated to an extraordinary session that took place after the official close of the council.[14] At the conclusion of this extraordinary session, Davis states,

> [T]he council fathers rejected the notion of an ecclesiastical coordinator or prefect apostolic. In fact, *nothing new was created to deal with the situation on a nationwide scale*. It was decided that each bishop who had blacks in his diocese would decide what was best and work in concert with others in the provincial synods.[15]

With this inaction, "a golden opportunity" had become a missed opportunity. Additionally, this marked an early occasion when church leaders in Rome displayed a genuine concern for African- descended people in the United

States when the bishops of the nation were unable to do so.[16]

It appears that the bishops attending this extraordinary session were unable to get out of their own way so that they could discern how to care for the spiritual and pastoral needs of the newly freed black Americans. The published decrees of the council are both telling and ominous. Davis cites them, 'The council decreed that it should "gravely weigh on our conscience that all might have access to draw near to Christ; that all who administer the sacraments might be present to all who seek them…" If 'through some stupidity' it should happen that this is not the case, 'one will merit the greatest opprobrium, who forgetful of his office, shall not offer the means of salvation to all who seek, whether black or other and who on account of this lack of care should perish [spiritually].'[17]

III Fall 2019 Meeting of the United States Conference of Catholic Bishops

One hundred fifty-three years after the Second Plenary Council of Baltimore, the United States Conference of Catholic Bishops (USCCB) gathered in Baltimore for their fall meeting. One of the most significant exchanges during this meeting centred on their provisional updated draft of the 2015 document, "Forming Consciences for Faithful Citizenship." At issue was an amendment brought to the floor by Cardinal Blase Cupich of Chicago to include paragraph 101 from Pope Francis's apostolic exhortation, *Gaudete et Exsultate*, (GE) in its entirety. It reads as follows:

> The other harmful ideological error is found in those who find suspect the social engagement of others, seeing it as superficial, worldly, secular, materialist, communist or populist. Or they relativize it, as if there are other more important matters, or the only thing that counts is one particular ethical issue or cause that they themselves defend. *Our defence of the innocent unborn, for example, needs to be clear, firm and passionate, for at stake is the dignity of a human life, which is always sacred and demands love for each person, regardless of his or her stage of development. Equally sacred, however, are the lives of the poor, those already born, the destitute, the abandoned and the underprivileged, the vulnerable infirm and elderly exposed to covert euthanasia, the victims of human trafficking, new forms of slavery, and every form of rejection.*

[84] We cannot uphold an ideal of holiness that would ignore injustice in a world where some revel, spend with abandon and live only for the latest consumer goods, even as others look on from afar, living their entire lives in abject poverty.[18]

Cupich's amendment attempted to amplify Pope Francis' wider teaching about human life being sacred in all its stages, with special attention to the poor and vulnerable. Nevertheless, the assembly of bishops rejected this amendment because some were apparently intent on not lengthening the document. According to historian and theologian, Massimo Faggioli, "the effort to neuter Pope Francis's message in the United States continues."[19] With these words, Faggioli was giving voice to a belief that the USCCB is at odds with Pope Francis. It is widely believed that bishops appointed by St. John Paul II and Pope Benedict are of a different ilk than those appointed by Pope Francis. While a footnote referencing the reader to paragraph 101 in GE was supposed to be included in the text, the difficulty, as some assess it, is the fact that the USCCB has made abortion their pre-eminent concern while Pope Francis has written about embracing a broader approach to life issues. Pope Francis could not have been more clear in paragraph 101 of GE as he spells out that all of life is sacred and that suffering humanity, especially, demands the church's compassionate response. These sisters and brothers are Schillebeeckx's threatened humanum in our midst and they deserve a prophetic and ethical response that makes clear that these circumstances should not be and must be changed.[20]

The failure of the U.S. bishops to incorporate the entire paragraph from GE is another missed "golden opportunity" to highlight the church's largesse and preferential option for the poor and vulnerable. The lives of these sisters and brothers are marked by struggle and are often cut short due to violence, poverty, and poor health care. When the U.S. bishops make abortion their "pre-eminent" life issue, it appears that they are perseverating on abortion and the so-called "fortnight for freedom" while they rarely write or speak on other social issues.

IV A Synodal Journey of Creativity and Responsibility

When speaking about the synodal process during an interview in 2013, Pope Francis affirmed, "We must walk together: the people, the bishops and the pope. Synodality should be lived at various levels."[21] In September 2018, the International Theological Commission (ITC) published the English translation of "Synodality in the Life and Mission of the Church." In it, the authors break open this neologism and explain its use over the recent decades. Rooted in Scripture and Tradition, this concept, like the church, is both ancient and new.

The ITC has indicated Pope Francis' role in the development of synodality and how he highlighted Blessed Paul VI's institution of the Synod of Bishops. Pope Francis has also explained that synodality is the path "which God expects of the Church of the third millennium."[22]

a) Creativity

Synodality and the path it opens can provide a space where the People of God can share "the joys and hopes, the griefs and the anxieties"[23] that they experience in a manner that can form community. Black Catholics and other marginalized Catholics want to know that their pope, bishops, sisters, and brothers are passionate about injustice "and will speak with urgency consistent with the depth of the wounds of the oppressed."[24]

In a compelling article Elissa Roper offers a refreshing explanation of what it means for the church to be synodal in "Synodality: A Process Committed to Transformation."[25] This transformation is about "journeying, creativity, and responsibility." When individuals are open to developing a new consciousness through "the renewing of their minds (Romans 12: 2)," it is a deepening of their baptismal call and their walk with Jesus Christ.[26] This transformation can enable our church community to face the stark reality of our institutional and personal involvement with racism, nativism, sexism, heterosexism, clericalism, and all types of exclusion. Then, we need only pivot to face the hard, cold, facts surrounding the global clergy sexual abuse scandal and cover-up as accusations continue to surface,[27] thus prompting our righteous indignation and passion "consistent with the depths of the wounds of the oppressed."

Synodality is a way of being in relationships where people can tell their stories of disappointment that their church community did not walk with them at moments of vulnerability, such as times past in the United States when black Catholic parishes were closed or when black Catholic individuals experienced discrimination in Catholic parishes, grades schools, or during Mass. We cannot forget the plight of displaced sisters and brothers at the southern border, who are now being taken to other Central American countries, to await assistance.

Creativity can happen along the synodal path as the faithful and their bishops speak frankly about their concerns and possible solutions. For instance, a parish community or entire diocese might form study circles based on Davis' *The History of Black Catholic in the United States*. This is important since the history of black Catholics is usually not included in histories of the Catholic Church in the United States. As long as members of the community are committed to listening to each other's stories, practices like these will move people toward a greater synodality.

More recently, the trend of closing or consolidating Offices of Black Catholic Ministry to be part of Offices of Multicultural Concerns, may cause one to wonder whether the concerns of black Catholics are being adequately promoted How might the void that has been created in neighbourhoods where Catholic parishes and schools once thrived be filled? Some congregations of women religious have opened study/learning centres for students or adults to provide opportunities for uplift. These concrete examples of being a presence and serving can be a powerful witness of the Catholic Church's concern for children and adults in struggling situations and/or neighbourhoods.

b) Responsibility
Roper maintains "[t]ransformation for a synodal Church at the universal level begins with an acknowledgment of the baptismal authority and responsibility of all members."[28] It is with this spirit that individuals and groups can come to terms with sins of omission and commission regarding the promotion of the Kingdom of God. Sins of racism, nativism, heterosexism, and clericalism are a good place to start where everyone can reflect upon their complicity against the backdrop of synodality and a commitment to walk with one's church community, even when it is uncomfortable.

One way of being responsible is by understanding one's social location, literally and figuratively. For instance, Baltimore is the first Catholic diocese in the United States. It is also a city plagued with a high murder rate, the opioid crisis, poor city management, the riots following the death of Freddie Gray in 2015, a history of housing discrimination and children suffering the long-term effects of lead poisoning.[29] Add to this, struggling public schools and the widening gap between the rich and the poor, and it is not hard to realize that this city cries out for justice. By being in tune with the location of their meetings, the bishops could very well allow this message to influence the spirit of the meeting. Something similar can be said for all of us. How can our social location have bearing on the choices we make and the things we spend time on?

III Conclusion

In this synodal spirit, all members of the church can journey together into our shared future ever mindful of the dangerous memory of sisters and brothers who have passed and those who walk with us still. The process of remembering them is a gift and a challenge as J. B. Metz would note:

> There are memories in which earlier experiences flare up and unleash new dangerous insights for the present. For brief moments they illuminate, harshly and piercingly, the problematic character of things we made our peace with a long time ago…Memories of this sort are dangerous and incalculable visitations from the past. They are memories that one has to take into account, memories that have a future content…[30]

May our church community have the courage to be faithful stewards of these unpredictable dangerous memories and to act upon them.

Bibliography

J. H. Cone, *A Black Theology of Liberation*, Twentieth Anniversary Edition, Maryknoll, NY: Orbis, 1986.

C. Davis and J. T. Phelps, *Stamped with the Image of God: African Americans as God's Image in Black (American Catholic Identities)*, Maryknoll, NY: Orbis, 2004.

C. Davis. *The History of Black Catholics in the United States*, New

York: Crossroad, 1990, 117.

M. Faggio. "Adrift and Alone: The Bishops Meet and Miss the Point", in *Commonweal*, November 25, 2019. https://www.commonwealmagazine.org/adrift-alone, Accessed on December 2, 2019.

Pope Francis, *A Big Heart Open to God: A Conversation with Pope Francis*, New York: HarperOne, 2013.

International Theological Commission. "Synodality in the Life and Mission of the Church," http://www.vatican.va/roman_curia/congregations/cfaith/cti_documents/rc_cti_20180302_sinodalita_en.html. Accessed on January 11, 2020.

J. Marbella, "Beginning of Freddie Gray's life as sad as its end, court case shows," in *The Baltimore Sun*, April 23, 2015.

J. B. Metz, *Faith in History and Society: Toward a Practical Fundamental Theology*, New York: Crossroad.

E. Schillebeeckx, Edward, *Christ the Christian Experience in the Modern World, The Collected Works of Edward Schillebeeckx*, Volume VII, New York: Bloomsbury, 2014.

Magisterial Documents:

Gaudium et Exultate, http://www.vatican.va/content/francesco/en/apost_exhortations/documents/papa-francesco_esortazione-ap_20180319_gaudete-et-exsultate.html, accessed on December 1, 2019.

Gaudium et Spes, http://www.vatican.va/archive/hist_councils/ii_vatican_council/documents/vat-ii_const_19651207_gaudium-et-spes_en.html. Accessed on January 11, 2020.

Notes

1. J. H. Cone, A Black Theology of Liberation, Twentieth Anniversary Edition, Maryknoll, NY: Orbis, 1986, p 17. Italics are mine.
2. Ibid.
3. Ibid.
4. B. N. Massingale, *Racial Justice and the Catholic Church*, Maryknoll, NY: Orbis, 2010, p 44.
5. Archbishop W. E. Lori of Baltimore has written two letters on racism. Bishop M. J. Seitz of El Paso wrote, "Night Shall Be No More." This letter on racism was a response to a mass shooting in that city on August 3, 2019 that targeted Latino/a people.

Passion Consistent With the Depth of the Wounds of the Oppressed

6. C. Davis and J. T. Phelps, *Stamped with the Image of God: African Americans as God's Image in Black (American Catholic Identities)*, Maryknoll, NY: Orbis, 2004.
7. C. Davis. *The History of Black Catholics in the United States*, New York: Crossroad, 1990, 117.
8. Ibid, 117.
9. Ibid, 118.
10. Ibid.
11. Ibid.
12. Ibid, 118.
13. Ibid, 119.
14. Ibid.
15. Ibid, 120. Italics are mine.
16. Ibid, 121.
17. Ibid.
18. *Gaudium et Exultate*. http://www.vatican.va/content/francesco/en/apost_exhortations/documents/papa-francesco_esortazione-ap_20180319_gaudete-et-exsultate.html, accessed on December 1, 2019. Italics are mine.
19. M. Faggio. "Adrift and Alone: The Bishops Meet and Miss the Point, in *Commonweal*, November 25, 2019. https://www.commonwealmagazine.org/adrift-alone, Accessed on December 2, 2019.
20. E. Schillebeeckx, Edward, *Christ the Christian Experience in the Modern World, The Collected Works of Edward Schillebeeckx*, Volume VII, New York: Bloomsbury, 2014, pp 649-659.
21. Pope Francis. *A Big Heart Open to God: A Conversation with Pope Francis*, New York: HarperOne, 2013, 39.
22. International Theological Commission. "Synodality in the Life and Mission of the Church," 1. http://www.vatican.va/roman_curia/congregations/cfaith/cti_documents/rc_cti_20180302_sinodalita_en.html. Accessed on January 11, 2020.
23. *Gaudium et Spes*, 1. http://www.vatican.va/archive/hist_councils/ii_vatican_council/documents/vat-ii_const_19651207_gaudium-et-spes_en.html. Accessed on January 11, 2020.
24. J. B. Metz, *Faith in History and Society: Toward a Practical Fundamental Theology*, New York: Crossroad, 105.
25. E. Roper, "Synodality: A Process Committed to Transformation. *The Australasian Catholic Record*, 95 no. 4, Oct. 2018, 412-423.
26. Ibid. 416.
27. Ibid. 416.
28. Freddie Gray and his siblings suffered from the long term effects of lead poisoning. See J. Marbella, "Beginning of Freddie Gray's life as sad as its end, court case shows," in *The Baltimore Sun*, April 23, 2015.
29. J. B. Metz, *Faith in History and Society: Toward a Practical Fundamental Theology*, New York: Crossroad, 105.

Theological Forum
Synodality – in Practice[1]

NORBERT METTE

Pope Francis is very anxious to see an enhancement of the status of synods as bodies for supporting decision-making processes in the Catholic Church, but there is disagreement about the status they should have within the hierarchical structure of the Church, about whether they should be an aid to consultation by the authorities on pending decisions or whether they should be able to make binding decisions. Perhaps the experiences of synods in the Catholic Church, by now going back almost 50 years, will be helpful in giving us insights into the factors that need to be taken into account for a constructive shaping of synodal processes.

Almost simultaneously, at the end of the 1960s and the beginning of the 1970s, meetings with a 'synodal character' took place in the Catholic Church in Europe, beginning with the 'Pastoral Council' in the Netherlands (1966-1970), followed by the 'Joint Synod of the Dioceses in the Federal Republic of Germany' (1971-1975), the 'Pastoral Synod of Jurisdictional Areas in the German Democratic Republic' (1973-1975), 'Synod 72' in Switzerland (1972-1975) and lastly the 'Austrian Synodal Process' (1973-1974). A common concern was, starting from the decisions of the Second Vatican Council, to take seriously the responsibility of the whole people of God for the mission of the Church, and to look for directions and signposts for a renewal of local Church life that would equip it to face the future. There was also a hope that the synods might make a contribution to reducing the tensions and conflicts that had emerged very soon after the Council between the supporters and opponents of reform.

What effects did these assemblies have on Church life in the various countries? And what can be learned from them about the development of a Church that takes its synodal character seriously, as Pope Francis wishes?[2] These were the main questions addressed by an international research project with the title 'Europe's National Synods after the Second Vatican Council' conducted under the leadership of Church historian Joachim Schmiedl of the Philosophical and Theological University of Vallendar (Germany) in cooperation with colleagues from various theological disciplines, whose findings were published in four volumes.[3] The first volume contains a new commentary on all the documents of the Joint Synod of the West German dioceses in the light of developments during the 40 years since the synods in the various subject areas. Volume 2 deals with the legal foundations of the synods of the period with an eye to any possibilities they offer for updating. The volume also looks at the status of synodal structures in the churches of the Reformation and the Orthodox churches. The question of the ecclesiological bases of local synodal assemblies is examined in Volume 3. The main question is the relationship between the Church leadership and the participation of the whole people of God in consultation and decision-making processes. A key element in the research project was the questioning of contemporary witnesses who took part in the synodal assemblies. The evaluation of their memories of the processes of the assemblies and the their assessment of the effects is presented in Volume 4. As noted, the five synodal assemblies mentioned in the introduction make up the centre of the research project. Only Arnaud Join-Lambert, a specialist in practical theology and liturgy from the Catholic University of Louvain-la-Neuve, takes a wider view with his international inventory of synods and – as he calls them – para-synods.[4] In addition, he looks at these meetings to see what problems have occurred in the Catholic Church in connection with these new consultation and decision-making processes and what questions they raise, especially for ecclesiology and canon law.

Taking the same approach, in this article I want, rather than to discuss in detail the individual synods examined in the research project or the methodology of the project, to summarise observations from the four volumes that, on the basis of the experiences of the synodal processes, highlight the possibilities and limitations of such a procedure in the Catholic Church.

First, it should be remembered that all these synodal assemblies took place during the validity of the 1917 Code of Canon Law. Under that code, for an assembly on the territory of several ecclesiastical provinces, the applicable regulations were those for a plenary council: permission from the Pope, summons and direction by a papal legate, only 'senior' members of the hierarchy to participate, ratification of decisions by the Apostolic See. After the Council the pressure for the calling of Church consultation and decision-making bodies came essentially from the Church grassroots. That meant – and to do so would also have contradicted the relevant statements of Vatican II – that it was impossible to exclude lay people from such assemblies. As a result, there was a search for ways in which canon law applicable at the time could be modified, whether to have an open consultation of bishops, priests, religious and laity without the power to make binding decisions, or a process of discussions with the Apostolic See in which statutes would be drafted and issued; under these the Vatican would accept a 'lay quorum', in other words, the participation of laity, with the right to vote, with the maximum number equal to the number of clergy. There was an exception in the case of the Joint Synod of the dioceses in the Federal Republic of Germany, for which a statute was negotiated with the Apostolic See. People like to see this as making a 'new type of synod' possible. The following were emphasised as the essential features: a pastoral outlook, not merely consultative, but also a having constitutive function for episcopal legislation (without reducing the bishops' competence), the expansion of participation to include laity and religious as full members (but with the 'lay quorum'), and a synod membership chosen on the principle of representativity.

One delicate point was the status of bishops within the synods. In principle, episcopal competence to legislate was recognised. The question was only whether and how far this power should or would be incorporated into the synodal process of consultation and decision-making. Here again different approaches were adopted: sometimes bishops did no more than listen to the debates and then draw their own conclusions. Sometimes they took an active part and argued their own position in the debates, thus making it clear how they would deal with the decisions taken. Whether the decisions, recommendations and regulations of the synods were applied in a particular diocese was (and is) under current canon law left to the discretion of the relevant bishop. On this point it is sobering to see that the closeness to or distance from their synod on the part of individual bishops turned out to be very varied.

On top of this comes the legal oversight of the Apostolic See, which is brought into play especially when issues are put on the agenda that are of significance for the universal Church. This had led to a situation in which such 'hot potatoes' as celibacy, *viri probati*, women deacons, and the remarriage of divorced people, were initially not approved for discussion, or the majority view emerging from the discussion at the synod was submitted to the Apostolic See as an 'opinion' or *votum*. The Vatican's overall restrictive attitude to these 'opinions' offended many synod members (and many others), not least because they saw it as disregarding the solemnly proclaimed 'whole people's discernment in matters of faith' (*Lumen Gentium* 12). As a result of this experience Join-Lambert called for 'an inductive reflection based on practice' about discernment in matters of faith.[5]

Join-Lambert's assessment of the post-conciliar synodal processes across the world led him to produce what he regarded as a typical four-stage model, though in view of the synods assessed in the research project this model needs to be slightly modified.

1)
There is an additional element in the form of a preliminary phase, in which a sense of urgency about the need to call a national synod develops. As noted above, this often starts with relevant pressure from the Church grassroots. Knowledge of synods or similar assemblies already taking place in other parts of the universal Church further reinforced the pressure from below. Sometimes the calling of an assembly at a national level was preceded by diocesan synods, though in Switzerland they took place simultaneously. Insights into the current state of opinion among the people of God gave further stimulus to the idea of calling a synod. In this connection it was found helpful, as shown by reports from the Netherlands and Switzerland,[6] to set up a local pastoral institute or institute of pastoral theology charged with constantly monitoring and analysing developments in society and the Church.

2)

Calling the synod and its work (stage 2, or 2 and 3 in Join-Lambert's model). After the decision to hold a synod was taken, normally by the bishops conference, the next step was to decide the procedure, through the drafting of legal regulations, deciding the length of time, identification of topics and appointments to commissions, etc. When the synod finally started to meet, the decisive processes took place in the plenary sessions. For these presentations on the topics were prepare in the meantime in the commissions and sub-groups. In addition to the internal debates, the involvement of the broader Church and general public had a considerable effect. Despite the workload involved for the participants by the number of sittings during this stage, participation in the synod is almost universally remembered as an extraordinary event.[7] An aspect that was felt to be particularly positive was the possibility to meet on equal terms. Even when on one topic or another there were arguments, overall the atmosphere was described as very constructive – this was helped in no small part by the possibilities of meeting informally over a meal or outside the sessions. Another factor was the incorporation of liturgies and prayers into the rhythm of the sessions and the physical surroundings, especially if the venue was a church. Many participants admitted that taking part in the synod had been a 'spiritual event' for them.

There were factors that influenced the course of the synods whose importance should not be underestimated: the role of protagonists who moved the consultations forward, the role of experienced speakers, who acquired supporter groups, the formation of informal groups and factions. For the significance of the synods beyond the circle of those immediately involved, their treatment in the media was important. Another group that was not without influence was the group of Church members that regarded the introduction of synodal elements into the Catholic Church as a betrayal of true Church teaching and therefore strove to thwart it by various means.

3)

Join-Lambert calls the last stage the 'closing phase', by which he means the solemn closure of the period of the synods' sessions. But that does not mean that the synodal process had come to an end.

4)
On the contrary, there now began a further crucial phase, that of the reception and effect of the synods. At the end there was a considerable quantity of documents. How were they dealt with? As a rule, they were published, sometimes with commentaries from the episcopal side. Some documents certainly had a lasting effect on the life of the Church.[8]

There was also an effort, mainly on the part of the bishops, to pack the synods away in the archives as quickly as possible. The appointment in the period after the synods of local bishops who had firmly rejected any sort of synodal processes in the Church reinforced the effort to let the synods be forgotten. An additional factor was the new Code of Canon Law, which, with its regulations for 'Particular Councils' (CIC/1983, cc. 439ff), showed no sign that the experiences of the synods that had been held had been taken into account. This led to a situation in which, apart from the holding of diocesan synods in a few places, a variety of forms for communal consultation of the people of God were 'invented' and transposed to diocesan or bishops conference level (Join-Lambert calls them 'para-synods') – as a rule with a consultative function as far as the diocesan bishop or bishops conference was concerned, who had complete discretion about how the 'suggestions' were handled. Participants in the earlier synods expressed disappointment 40 years later that the 'difficult issues' of those days had not been dealt with and were still on the Church's agenda, quite apart from issues that had emerged in the meantime.[9] Many Catholic Christians who had been involved in the reform process for a long period have since given up and withdrawn and sometimes now invest their energy in what they feel are more important and 'more worthwhile' areas of society.

The crucial question as we look to the future will be how synodal elements in the Catholic Church get along with its hierarchical structure, which reserves the right of final decision to the Church leadership. The possibilities for progress here offered by post-conciliar ecclesiology are discussed in the third volume. One thing is clear: if synodal life is (once more) to become a structural principle in the Catholic Church as in others, as canon lawyer Sabine Demel insists forcefully,[10] a thoroughgoing change will be required in the theological understanding of offices in the Church and how they are exercised pastorally – and this will have to include canonical rules. Pope Francis' moves in this direction give hope.11 Nonetheless the internal Church opposition he attracts, not least because of this, is also a fact, and it is still to early to see what its effect will be.

Translated by Francis McDonagh

Notes

1. Cf International Theological Commission, Synodality in the Life and Mission of the Church, 2 March 2018: http://www.vatican.va/roman_curia/congregations/cfaith/cti_documents/rc_cti_20180302_sinodalita_en.html
2. See especially Pope Francis, *Address to the Ceremony Commemorating the 50th Anniversary of the Institution of the Synod of Bishops*, 17 October 2015: http://w2.vatican.va/content/francesco/en/speeches/2015/october/documents/papa-francesco_20151017_50-anniversario-sinodo.html
3. Cf Reinhard Feiter, Richard Hartmann and Joachim Schmiedl (ed.), *Die Würzburger Synode. Texte neu gelesen* (Europas Synoden nach dem Zweiten Vatikanischen Konzil vol. 1), (Freiburg im Breisgau, 2013); Wilhelm Rees and Joachim Schmiedl (ed.), *Unverbindliche Beratung oder kollegiale Steuerung? Kirchenrechtliche Überlegungen zu synodalen Vorgängen* (vol. 2) (Freiburg am Breisgau, 2014); Joachim Schmiedl and Robert Walz (ed.), *Die Kirchenbilder der Synoden. Zur Umsetzung konziliarer Ekklesiogie in teilkirchlichen Strukturen* (Bd. 3) (Freiburg am Breisgau, 2015); Joachim Schmiedl and Wilhelm Rees (ed.), *Die Erinnerung an die Synoden. Ereignis und Deutung – in Interviews nachgefragt* (Bd. 4), (Freiburg am Breisgau, 2017).
4. Cf Rees and Schmiedl, *Unverbindliche Beratung oder kollegiale Steuerung?*
5. Rees and Schmiedl, *Unverbindliche Beratung oder kollegiale Steuerung?*, p.280.
6. Cf Schmiedl and Walz, *Die Kirchenbilder der Synoden.*
7. Schmiedl and Rees, *Die Erinnerung an die Synoden.*
8. A participant in the pastoral synod in the German Democratic Republic describes this Church meeting as having in addition a 'particular effect in giving training in the skills of democracy in a non-democratic state' (quoted in Schmiedl and Rees).
9. See Schmiedl and Rees.
10. See Schmiedl and Walz, *Die Kirchenbilder der Synoden.*
11. See, in addition to Pope Francis's address before the 2015 synod (above, note 2), and his Apostolic Exhortation *Evangelii Gaudium* – that is fundamental – his address to the Italian bishops conference on 20 May 2019: http://w2.vatican.va/content/francesco/it/speeches/2019/may/documents/papa-francesco_20190520_cei.html and his letter to 'the pilgrim people of God in Germany' of 29 June 2019: http://w2.vatican.va/content/francesco/de/letters/2019/documents/papa-francesco_20190629_lettera-fedeligermania.html

Contributors

JOHN D. CAPUTO, the Watson Professor of Religion Emeritus (Syracuse University) and the Cook Professor of Philosophy Emeritus (Villanova University) is a constructive theologian who works in the area of "weak" or "radical" theology. His majors works include *Radical Hermeneutics* (1987), *The Prayers and Tears of Jacques Derrida* (1997), *The Weakness of God* (2006). His most recent works are *Hermeneutics: Facts and Interpretation in the Age of Information* (2018) and a second edition of *On Religion* (2018). *The Essential Caputo* (2018) a collection of his work from the early 1970s on. His latest books are *Cross and Cosmos: A Theology of Difficult Glory* (2019) and *Radical Theology*, forthcoming in 2020. He has addressed more general audiences in books like *What Would Jesus Deconstruct?* (2006) and *Hoping against Hope* (2015).

Address: Thomas J. Watson Professor Emeritus of Religion, Syracuse University, David R. Cook Professor Emeritus of Philosophy, Villanova University, 800 Lancaster Avenue, Villanova, PA 19085, USA

JOÃO J. VILA-CHÃ is a Portuguese Jesuit and Professor for Social and Political Philosophy at the Pontifical Gregorian University in Rome. He is member of the Editorial Board of Concilium and of the Steering Committee of the International Federation of Philosophical Societies (FISP). He is also President of COMIUCAP and Vice-President of the Council for Research in Values and Philosophy (Washington, DC).

Address: Pontificia Università Gregoriana, Piazza della Pilotta, 4, 00187 ROMA, ITALY
Email : j.vila-cha@unigre.it

IVONI RICHTER REIMER - PhD in Philosophy/Theology from Universitaet Kassel; Professor at the Pontifical Catholic University of Goiás. Lutheran theologian.

Contributors

Email: ivonirr@gmail.com

HAROLDO REIMER – Doctor of Theology from Kirchliche Hochschule Bethel; Professor at the State University of Goiás. Lutheran theologian.
Email: haroldo.reimer@gmail.com

MARIA ARUL RAJA – Dr. A. Maria Arul Raja SJ is the Director of the IDCR (Institute of Dialogue with Cultures and Religions)- Loyola College- Chennai for the doctoral studies on Comparative Religions and Cultures affiliated to Madras University. Teaching Scripture, Theology, and Religious Studies from 1993 onwards in various centres of higher learning, he served in Arul Kadal Jesuit Theology Centre-Chennai as the Dean of Studies for 20 years. His interdisciplinary and subaltern insights have been published in his 10 books and over 160 research articles in international and national journals. He has lectured and presented papers both in the West and the East while continuing his dialogical engagement with People's Movements and Marginalized groups.
Email: amarajasj@gmail.com

DR JUDITH HAHN, BPhil, has a doctorate in theology and a licenciate in canon law. She is professor of canon law in the Faculty of Catholic Theology at Ruhr University Bochum. She has published extensively on the theory and sociology of canon law, on religious law and legal pluralism, and on the status of the church and its law in the Western states and modern societies. Her most recent books are: *Church Law in Modernity: Toward a Theory of Canon Law between Nature and Culture*, Cambridge University Press: Cambridge, 2019, and *Grundlegung der Kirchenrechtssoziologie*, Springer: Wiesbaden, 2019.
Email: judith.hahn@rub.de

HILLE HAKER, Ph.D., holds the Richard McCormick S.J. Endowed Chair of Catholic Moral Theology at Loyola University Chicago. Her research focuses on the foundations of ethics, moral identity, literary & narrative ethics, social and political ethics, bioethics, and feminist ethics. Recent books are: *The Renewal of Catholic Social ethics. Towards a Critical Political Ethics*. Würzburg: Echter, 2020, and *Unaccompanied*

Migrant Children. Social, Legal, and Ethical Perspectives. Lanham, MD: Lexington, 2019 (co-edited with Molly Greening).
 Address: Prof. Dr. Hille Haker, Richard McCormick Endowed Chair of Ethics, Loyola University Chicago, Theology Department, Crown Center 319, 1032 W. Sheridan Rd, Chicago, Il, 60660,
 Email: hhaker@luc.edu

PROF. DR. ANSGAR KREUTZER, studying Catholic theology, sociology and the philosophy of religion in Freiburg / Br., Paris and Frankfurt / M., 2011–2017 he was professor of fundamental theology and head of the newly founded department for religious studies at the Catholic Private University Linz. Since 2017 he has been Professor of Systematic Theology at the Institute for Catholic Theology at the Justus Liebig University Gießen. Main focus of his work is the Theology of the Second Vatican Council; Theology of kenosis; and Political theologies.
 Email: ansgar.kreutzer@katheologie.uni-giessen.de

FRANCISCO DA AQUINO JÚNIOR — Doctor of Theology, Westfälischen Wilhelms-Universität, Münster – Germany; Professor of Theology, Faculdade Católica de Fortaleza (FCF) and of the Universidade Católica de Pernambuco (UNICAP); priest in the Diocese of Limoeiro do Norte – CE – Brasil.
 Email: axejun@yahoo.com.br;
 Orcid: http://orcid.org/0000-0001-8142-3280.

DR TANYA VAN WYK is Senior Lecturer in Spirituality, Systematic Theology and Ethics at the Faculty of Theology and Religion, University of Pretoria. Her research focuses on political theology and the relationship between identity and diversity, by utilizing perspectives from trinitarian theology, feminist theology and spirituality-studies. She is an ordained minister of the Netherdutch Reformed Church.
 Address: Faculty of Theology and Religion, University Of Pretoria Lynnwood Road Pretoria, Pretoria, South Africa
 Telephone: + (27) 82 774 7907
 Email: tanya.vanwyk@up.ac.za

Contributors

JOSE MARIO C. FRANCISCO — is a Filipino Jesuit Professor at Loyola School of Theology, Ateneo de Manila University. He has taught at other institutions in the Philippines and abroad; among them, East Asian Pastoral Institute, Gregorian University and Boston College. His research deals with the interface between theology and cultural studies in Asian Christianity. He has published in *Concilium* and other international journals as well as in books like *The Oxford Handbook of Asian Christianity*. He is on the editorial board of *The International Journal of Asian Christianity and Asia Pacific Mission Studies*.
  Address: Ateneo de Manila University, Quezon City, Philippines
  Email: jmfrancisco@ateneo.edu

LaREINE-MARIE MOSELY, SND — is a tenured Associate Professor of Theology at Notre Dame of Maryland University in Baltimore, MD, a small women's college with a diverse student population. She received her PhD in systematic theology from the University of Notre Dame where she wrote her dissertation on womanist and black feminist perspectives on the cross of Jesus Christ in the later soteriology of Edward Schillebeeckx. She is a member of the German branch of the Sisters of Notre Dame. Her research interests include soteriology, womanist theology, black theology, black Catholic theology, interculturality and religious life, and theologies of Mary.
  Addres: The Sisters of Notre Dame Center, 5900 Davis Road, Whitehouse, Ohio 43571.
  Email: lmosely@toledosnd.org

NORBERT METTE was professor of religious education and pastoral theology at the universities of Paderborn and Dortmund (Germany). He retired in 2011. His latest publication is: *Nicht gleichgültig bleiben! Die soziale Botschaft von Papst Franziskus*, Ostfildern 2018.
  Address: Liebigweg 11a, D-48165 Münster
  Email: norbert.mette@freenet.de

CONCILIUM
International Journal of Theology

FOUNDERS

Anton van den Boogaard; Paul Brand; Yves Congar, OP; Hans Küng;
Johann Baptist Metz; Karl Rahner, SJ; Edward Schillebeeckx

BOARD OF DIRECTORS

President: Thierry-Marie Courau OP
Vice-Presidents: Susan Abraham, Carlos Mendoza-Álvarez OP,
Stefanie Knauss, Daniel Franklin Pilario CM

BOARD OF EDITORS

Susan Abraham, Los Angeles (USA)
Michel Andraos, Chicago (USA)
Antony John Baptist, Bangalore (India)
Michelle Becka, Würzburg (Deutschland)
Sharon A. Bong, Selangor (Malaysia)
Bernadeth Caero Bustillos, Osnabrück (Deutschland)
Catherine Cornille, Boston (USA)
Thierry-Marie Courau OP, Paris (France)
Geraldo Luiz De Mori SJ, Belo Horizonte (Brasil)
Margareta Gruber OSF, Vallendar (Deutschland)
Stan Chu Ilo, Chicago (USA)
Huang Po-Ho, Tainan (Taiwan)
Stefanie Knauss, Villanova (USA)
Guztáv Kovács, Pécs (Magyarország)
Carlos Mendoza-Álvarez OP, Ciudad de México (México)
Esther Mombo, Limuru (Kenya)
Gianluca Montaldi, Brescia (Italia)
Daniel Franklin Pilario CM, Quezon City (Filipinas)
Carlos Schickendantz, Santiago (Chile)
Stephan van Erp, Leuven (Belgium)

PUBLISHERS

Hymns Ancient & Modern (London, UK)
Matthias-Grünewald Verlag (Ostfildern, Germany)
Editrice Queriniana (Brescia, Italy)
Editorial Verbo Divino (Estella, Spain)
EditoraVozes (Petropolis, Brazil)

Concilium Secretariat:

Couvent de l'Annonciation
222 rue du Faubourg Saint-Honoré
75008 – Paris (France)
secretariat.concilium@gmail.com
Managing Editor: Gianluca Montaldi FN
https://concilium-vatican2.org

Concilium Subscription Information

October   **2020/4:** *Signs of Hope for Muslim-Christian Dialogue*

December   **2020/5:** *Differently Able: for a Church Where All Belong*

February   **2021/1:** *Church in the Borders*

April   **2021/2:** *Synodality*

July   **2021/3:** *Incarnation*

New subscribers: to receive the next five issues of Concilium *please copy this form, complete it in block capitals and send it with your payment to the address below. Alternatively subscribe online at www.conciliumjournal.co.uk*

Please enter my annual subscription for *Concilium* starting with issue 2020/3.

Individuals
____ £52 UK
____ £75 overseas and (Euro €92, US $110)

Institutions
____ £75 UK
____ £95 overseas and (Euro €120, US $145)

Postage included – airmail for overseas subscribers

Payment Details:
Payment can be made by cheque (£ Sterling only), by credit/debit card or bank transfer.
a. I enclose a cheque for £ _____ Payable to Hymns Ancient and Modern Ltd
b. To pay by Visa/Mastercard please contact us on +44(0)1603 785911 or go to www.conciliumjournal.co.uk
c. To pay in US $ or Euro € by bank transfer please contact us on +44(0)1603 785911

Contact Details:

Name ....

Address ....

....

Telephone .... E-mail ....

Send your order to *Concilium,* **Hymns Ancient and Modern Ltd**
13a Hellesdon Park Road, Norwich NR6 5DR, UK
E-mail: concilium@hymnsam.co.uk
or order online at www.conciliumjournal.co.uk

Customer service information
All orders must be prepaid. Your subscription will begin with the next issue of Concilium. *If you have any queries or require Information about other payment methods, please contact our Customer Services department.*

The Canterbury Dictionary of HYMNOLOGY — The result of over ten years of research by an international team of editors, The Canterbury Dictionary of Hymnology is the major online reference work on hymns, hymn-writers and traditions.

www.hymnology.co.uk

CHURCH TIMES — The Church Times, founded in 1863, has become the world's leading Anglican newspaper. It offers professional reporting of UK and international church news, in-depth features on faith, arts and culture, wide-ranging comment and all the latest clergy jobs. Available in print and online.

www.churchtimes.co.uk

Crucible — Crucible is the Christian journal of social ethics. It is produced quarterly, pulling together some of the best practitioners, thinkers, and theologians in the field. Each issue reflects theologically on a key theme of political, social, cultural, or environmental significance.

www.cruciblejournal.co.uk

JLS — Joint Liturgical Studies offers a valuable contribution to the study of liturgy. Each issue considers a particular aspect of liturgical development, such as the origins of the Roman rite, Anglican Orders, welcoming the Baptised, and Anglican Missals.

www.jointliturgicalstudies.co.uk

magnet — Magnet is a resource magazine published three times a year. Packed with ideas for worship, inspiring artwork and stories of faith and justice from around the world.

www.ourmagnet.co.uk

For more information on these publications visit the websites listed above or contact **Hymns Ancient & Modern**:
Tel.: +44 (0)1603 785 910
Write to: Subscriptions, Hymns Ancient & Modern,
13a Hellesdon Park Road, Norwich NR6 5DR

www.ingramcontent.com/pod-product-compliance
Ingram Content Group UK Ltd.
Pitfield, Milton Keynes, MK11 3LW, UK
UKHW042006230426
12048UKWH00009B/592